THE JOY OF

Ice Cream

MATTHEW KLEIN

BARRON'S

Woodbury, New York • London • Toronto • Sydney

Design by Milton Glaser, Inc.
Color Photographs by Matthew Klein
Helen Feingold, food stylist
Linda Cheverton, prop stylist

We are grateful to the following sources for
supplying props for the photographs in this book:
Limoges Porcelain by Cerelain from Baccarat;
sterling silver flatware and accessories from
Buccellati; crystal bowls from Baccarat, all of New
York City.

All inquiries should be addressed to:
Barron's Educational Series, Inc.
113 Crossways Park Drive
Woodbury, New York 11797

International Standard Book No. 0-8120-5630-2
Library of Congress No. 85-3846

Library of Congress Cataloging in Publication Data

Klein, Matthew.
  The joy of ice cream.

  Includes index.
  1. Ice cream, ices, etc.   I. Title.
TX795.K55   1985   641.8'62   85-3846
ISBN 0-8120-5630-2

PRINTED IN THE UNITED STATES OF AMERICA

5 6 7 8   790   9 8 7 6 5 4 3 2 1

Contents

Introduction

Ice cream is indeed a joy. There's nothing bad about ice cream. No one I've ever known has become saddened from eating ice cream. It is never disappointing.

I suppose it's the very positive nature of ice cream that intrigues me. Ice cream is a known positive experience. It is happy food, whether it's a double-scoop cone enjoyed in the park or an elaborate frozen concoction in an elegant restaurant.

Ice cream has a diversity of expression unmatched by any other food. Though its foundations are simple, it adapts to unlimited variations. With vanilla ice cream as a base, you can let loose your gustatory imagination and develop endless flavors and combinations.

It is fun to make your own ice cream, and it is also fun to use ice cream as an ingredient for making sodas, sundaes, cakes, pies, and other desserts. This book tells you first of all how to make your own ice cream—probably the best ice cream you'll ever eat. Then it gives you a variety of sodas and sundaes to make with ice cream, whether you've made that ice cream or purchased a commercial type. The sodas and sundaes are a blending of the old favorites and some new ideas, as are the recipes that follow for cakes, pies, ice cream bombes, and other frozen desserts. None of the recipes in this book is terribly difficult; in fact, they are almost all surprisingly easy.

I urge you to try the recipes for my favorite ice cream flavors, then move on to develop your own flavors. You'll soon see how a few simple elements work together to produce America's favorite food. You too can experience the *Joy of Ice Cream.*

About Ice Cream

Ice cream is a simple combination of milk products, sweetenings, and flavorings. There are basically two kinds of ice cream: Philadelphia-style, which is made with various combinations of milk, cream, flavorings, and sugar; and custard-based, which is made with egg yolks, sugar, some milk, a lesser amount of cream, and similar flavorings. Custard ice creams, sometimes called French ice creams, are whipped before they are frozen. With the exception of the egg yolks in the custard ice cream, basically the ingredients for both are the same, although the proportions are different.

The Importance of Butterfat

We all love ice cream that is smooth and velvety. Ice cream has to contain a certain amount of butterfat to be so smooth. The butterfat in ice cream comes from the milk products in the mixture, and the higher the butterfat content, the richer the ice cream. The amount of butterfat in commercial ice cream is regulated by the F.D.A. For vanilla ice cream, the standard is at least 10 percent; for chocolate ice cream, it is at least 8 percent. Many ice creams that you buy in the store barely reach that minimum, while others reach 15 to 20 percent. If you make your own ice cream, you can increase the butterfat content even more, resulting in the smoothest ice cream you'll ever eat.

The recipes in this book all use high quantities of cream. There are three cups of heavy cream and one cup of half-and-half in most of the Philadelphia ice cream recipes. There are two cups of heavy cream, one cup of half-and-half, and four egg yolks in each of the custard ice cream recipes. These recipes will yield ice cream that far surpasses any of the commercial brands, some of which substitute chemical additives, gelatin, and other stabilizers to provide smoothness and body.

Smoothness in ice cream is achieved only with some sacrifice. That same butterfat that makes the ice cream so tasty also can be a problem for people with high cholesterol levels. You could reduce the amount of butterfat in the ice cream by substituting half-and-half for the cream and milk for the half-and-half. The problem is that you'll get an icier ice cream. The ice cream just won't be as smooth. It tends, especially in home units, to become very granular when there's too much water and not enough fat in the mixture. If you want smoothness, the only solution I can recommend is to eat very, very good ice cream—and only eat a little bit. Ice cream that's well made (or anything else, for that matter) need not be eaten to excess to be satisfying. In France they serve ice cream in tiny cones. The cones are perhaps an inch and a half in diameter at the widest point. They are perfectly satisfying. It's exactly right; the ice cream hits the spot.

Overrun

If you simply mixed up a batch of cream, sugar, and flavorings and then froze it, you would get a solid block that you'd have to chip at with an icepick. The mixture has to be aerated as it freezes to blend in that second most important factor in making good ice cream: air. The air lightens the mixture and increases its volume while keeping the cream soft. Too little air makes a solid ice cream; too much air gives you frozen foam.

Commercial manufacturers often use an air pump, which pumps air into the mixture as it is being frozen. Home ice cream machines do a similar thing by stirring a small amount of air into the mixture as it freezes. You can control to some extent the amount of air being incorporated and thus control the density of your ice cream (see pages 6–9). There are some recipes for ice creams made only in a freezer tray, for which you stir the mixture every so often to break up the ice crystals as it freezes, but these ice creams are inferior to those made in an ice cream freezer and we have not included recipes for them in this book.

The percentage of air that is whipped into ice cream is referred to as its overrun. The F.D.A. has standards for the weight of ice cream, and these weights are a direct reflection of overrun. A gallon of commercial ice cream must weigh at least 4.5 pounds, but in contrast, the ice cream you make at home will weigh twice that. Some popular brands of ice cream advertise a low overrun; Godiva and Häagen-Dazs, for example, have 20 percent overruns, meaning that for every 100 ounces of cream mixture, they beat in enough air to produce 120 ounces of frozen ice cream. A 20 percent overrun is very good; many ice creams have much higher overruns; Baskin-Robbins, for example, claims a 50 percent overrun, which means the ice cream is one-third air. Try this: hold up two different containers of ice cream at once and notice which is heavier. The heavier one has the lower overrun, which means you're getting more ice cream and less air for your money.

Ingredients

It pays to use only the freshest, best ingredients. Why spend all that time and effort to make something that is second rate? If you want second-rate ice cream, you can find that easily. And along with second-rate taste, you'll get homogenizers, stabilizers, and emulsifiers; corn syrups instead of sugar; and artificial flavors instead of real flavors.

In addition to wanting your efforts to go into the best possible results, be aware that the freezing process tends to bring out all the imperfections in ingredients. If you compromise on quality, you'll taste it.

Lastly, remember that in making ice cream you are working with cream and eggs, two food items that when not in top condition can have extremely high bacteria counts. This means that if anything is spoiled, it tends to spoil the rest of the mixture. It's healthier to use the freshest ingredients you can find.

In addition to the freshest cream, half-and-half, and eggs, you should be using only real vanilla extract. The vanilla extract reinforces the flavor of the cream and gives the ice cream its characteristic dairy taste. Imitation vanilla just doesn't do the job, and it lends a metallic aftertaste.

Chocolate should be pure and of top quality. Use reliable brands such as Hershey's or more expensive European chocolates like Lindt, Tobler, or—my favorites—Callibaut or Cote d'Or. For cocoa, use top-quality powders with a fine grind. The Dutch-process cocoas like Van Houten or Dröste are very good.

The fruits you use should be very fresh. If strawberries or raspberries aren't in season, think twice about making strawberry or raspberry ice cream. Or, if you can't wait for summer, substitute good, quick-frozen fruits and then drain off all the sugar syrup. Actually, since most people want to make fruit-flavored ice creams when the fruits are at their peak, it shouldn't be a problem.

5

All the nuts going into ice cream should be unsalted. Raisins should be plumped in hot water or another liquid before being added to ice cream. If desired, you can stir in commercial chocolate morsels, but you might find that making your own chips produces ice cream that's more fun to eat. For variety, consider stirring in fresh candy bits or crisp cookie crumbs. Most of these are added just before the ice cream is packed for hardening in the freezer; see individual recipes for instructions.

Ice Cream Machines

Ice cream is made by stirring the cream mixture while it freezes. The mixture has to be stirred constantly and not too quickly, but at a pace that allows the cream to freeze without becoming solid and without separating. For the home, there are basically only a few kinds of machines. Each has its advantages, but also its disadvantages.

The hand-cranked machine is essentially a canister that is held within a larger bucket. By turning the crank, you are able to turn the canister, which has a beater, or dasher, inside it to stir the cream. Between the canister and the bucket, you pack in layers of ice and salt. The salt keeps the ice cold and actually lowers the temperature of the ice while melting it, thus making a very cold sheath around the canister to help freeze the cream.

To freeze the cream, you begin cranking and keep on cranking until the handle is extremely hard to turn. The turning becomes difficult partly because of fatigue but mostly because the mixture becomes thickened as it freezes. At that point, the ice cream is ready, but that usually takes about half an hour. (But it seems like an hour and a half.)

For the hand-cranked machine, it is important to remember that the finer the ice particles you use, the smoother the ice cream that will result. Shaved ice is best, but it is difficult to find. A fine-grained salt is better than coarse salt, too, because it dissolves more quickly, lowering the temperature of the ice. There are several manufacturers of hand-cranked machines (White Mountain and Richmond Cedar Works, for example), and they are great if you want the nostalgia of ice-cream making. I don't recommend these, however, because I think they are just too much work.

Motor-driven machines are basically the same as hand-cranked machines except that the mixture is turned with a motor while you're busy cleaning up the mess you've made in the kitchen. There are several excellent brands on the market, including ones by White Mountain and Richmond Cedar Works. In fact, Richmond makes several types, some with wooden buckets and some with plastic buckets, in various sizes. The plastic bucket is easier to clean and the smaller ones are easiest to store for those occasional times when you won't be making ice cream.

The Waring Ice Cream Parlor is a simple, compact machine that has been rated tops in many comparative studies of ice cream freezers, both for the quality of the ice cream it produces and its relatively low price (about $40). The Waring is a modification of the motor-driven bucket model, in a sleeker upright design whose canister sits above the motor unit. It uses ice cubes and table salt—two items easily found in most kitchens. In about thirty minutes, the ice cream is ready to be packed for hardening. For this machine, as well as for the bucket types, the less salt you use, the finer the ice cream. Don't use more than half a box of salt. One note of caution: many of these recipes require adding some ingredients after the freezing process is well under way. If you use a salt-and-ice machine, you must be very careful not to allow any of the ice salt to get into the ice cream during this step.

If you don't want to bother with the salt and ice, then the Salton Ice Cream Machine is a possible option. This machine is simply filled with the cream mixture and placed in the freezer section of your refrigerator. The cord has to extend out of the freezer and you need to have an outlet nearby. The ice cream is grainy, but the processing is very easy.

There is yet another type of machine available. This is the self-freezing variety, with a canister inside the machine itself and with the freezing coils wrapped around the canister. The cream mixture is stirred inside the canister as it is frozen, without need for salt or ice. These units are expensive, averaging about $400. There are a couple of brands on the market, but the one I prefer is the Simac Gelataio. Until recently, the Simac canister wasn't removable for cleaning, but that has been corrected. The one difficulty of this machine is that the freezing coils must be kept upright. In fact, be sure when you buy your Gelataio that you carry the package home with you always in an upright position. If shifted on its side, the machine will not function; the freezing element in the coils is affected.

There's another popular self-freezing unit called the Minigel. This machine is handmade in Italy and is even more costly than the Simac. It makes a quart of top-quality ice cream in 15 to 20 minutes, making this the preferred unit for many restaurants. Minigel is available by mail order from Williams-Sonoma, P.O. Box 7456, San Francisco, CA 94120.

The big advantage of the self-freezing machines is that they are virtually foolproof. You just can't make a mistake. You can't have a grainy ice cream. You can't have water condensation unless your mixture is improper. They make delicious, top-quality ice cream with little fuss or bother.

Packing it Away

Some people like to eat the ice cream right from the canister or bucket. Others like to chill it to make it quite hard. When ice cream comes from the machine, regardless of the type of machine, it is light and fluffy. When you pack it in containers to store in the freezer, it hardens but if your recipe is good, the ice cream should remain creamy and smooth. The best storage for ice cream is about 0°. Pack it tightly in airtight containers and top the ice cream with a layer of plastic, tapping it down to cover the surface. Place the container cover on top and label the ice cream as to flavor and date.

When you are ready to serve your ice cream, take it out of the freezer and place in the refrigerator for about 15 minutes to soften slightly. If you are making scoops of ice cream, dip the scoop into tepid water and shake the moisture off. Dip again between scoops. If you are using the ice cream to make ice cream cakes or pies or other desserts, you'll have to soften the ice cream enough to shape it as desired, then freeze it again to retain the shape. Often you'll have to refreeze for up to 3 or 4 hours to get it really firm. If you are coating the ice cream with chocolate or covering it with meringue (as in Baked Alaska), the ice cream must be *very* firm.

Commercial Ice Creams

I've said a lot of nasty things about commercial ice creams, yet I know that there are times when people will want to forego making their own ice cream. If you are buying commercial ice cream, you can make a few comparisons to find ice cream that's almost as good as homemade. First off, read the label. Years ago, there weren't labels that listed ingredients, but nowadays you can use the listing to find out a little about the contents before purchasing. Look for ice creams that list cream as the first ingredient, for these will have the highest butterfat content, and thus the richest ice cream. Avoid those that list corn syrup instead of sugar and also eliminate any that list artificial colors or flavors. Try the heft comparison described on page 4 to determine the overrun.

Once you've purchased the ice cream, taste it. If you bought vanilla (the stiffest test of quality), the vanilla flavor should balance with the taste of cream, and the overall affect shouldn't be too sweet. Many commercial ice creams try to cover up flaws with sugar. With other flavors, the particular flavor should predominate but the taste of cream itself should still be there. Regardless of flavor, the texture of the ice cream should be smooth, not grainy or with ice bits.

Ice Cream Flavors

Old-Fashioned Vanilla

Ingredients

1 large egg
1 cup half-and-half
¾ cup granulated sugar

1 Tb. vanilla extract
3 cups heavy cream

Preparation

Put the egg, half-and-half, sugar, and vanilla extract in a blender, and blend on medium speed until the mixture is smooth and sugar is dissolved. Slowly add the cream and continue blending on low speed until mixture is smooth, about 30 seconds.

Transfer the mixture to your ice-cream machine and freeze according to manufacturer's instructions.

Makes slightly more than 1 quart

Photo 3 following page 42

Vanilla Malted

Ingredients

1 Tb. malted milk powder
1 large egg
1 cup half-and-half

¾ cup granulated sugar
1 Tb. vanilla extract
3 cups heavy cream

Preparation

Put the malted milk powder, egg, half-and-half, sugar, and vanilla extract in a blender, and blend on medium speed until the mixture is smooth and sugar is dissolved. Slowly add the cream and continue blending on low speed until mixture is smooth, about 30 seconds.

Transfer the mixture to your ice-cream machine, and freeze according to manufacturer's instructions.

Makes slightly more than 1 quart

Rich Vanilla Custard

Ingredients

1 vanilla bean, cut in
   $1/4$-inch pieces
$3/4$ cup granulated sugar
5 large egg yolks
1 cup half-and-half
2 cups well-chilled heavy
   cream
dash of salt

Preparation

Place the vanilla bean and sugar in a blender or food processor fitted with a steel blade, and chop the bean until it is in small bits. Set aside.

Place the egg yolks in a large mixing bowl, and beat with an electric hand mixer until foamy and light colored. Add the half-and-half and the vanilla-flavored sugar. Set the bowl over a saucepan filled with hot water and beat the egg and cream mixture until thickened and about double its original volume, about 10 minutes.

Remove bowl from the heat and immediately place into a larger bowl filled with ice cubes. Beat the mixture steadily until it is no longer warm. Add the cream and salt, and continue to beat until quite smooth. Transfer the cream mixture to your ice-cream machine and freeze according to the manufacturer's instructions.

Makes about 1 quart

Variations • Vanilla Fudge

1 cup Chocolate Fudge Sauce (page 189)

When the ice cream has frozen to the consistency of sour cream (or slightly harder), spoon the mixture out of the machine container and place about a 1-inch layer of it into your freezer container. Cover the ice cream with a thin (⅛-inch) layer of the fudge sauce. Add another layer of ice cream about 1 inch thick, then another layer of fudge sauce. Continue until all the fudge sauce and all the ice cream are in the freezer container. Stir *once* with a wooden spoon, pulling the

Variation • Nuts!

¾ cup chopped mixed unsalted nuts

When the ice cream is almost frozen but still turning in the ice-cream machine, add the nuts and continue freezing.

Vanilla-Lover's Vanilla

Ingredients

1 large egg
¾ cup extrafine sugar
4 cups heavy cream

1½ Tb. vanilla extract

Preparation

Put the egg, sugar, 2 cups heavy cream, and vanilla extract in a blender, and blend on medium speed until dissolved. Add the remaining cream and blend on low speed until smooth, about 30 seconds.

Transfer the mixture to your ice-cream machine and proceed according to the manufacturer's instructions.

Makes about 1 quart

Lemon Vanilla

Ingredients

1 vanilla bean
1 cup half-and-half
6 Tb. granulated sugar
4 pieces (3 × ½ inch)
  lemon rind, yellow part
  only

2 tsp. vanilla extract
½ tsp. fresh lemon juice
3 cups heavy cream

Preparation

Split the vanilla bean lengthwise in half and scrape the seeds into a small saucepan. Add the bean pod, half-and-half, sugar, and lemon rind. Set over moderate heat and bring to foaming (near-boil), stirring to dissolve the sugar. Remove from heat, cover, and let steep until cool.

Strain the cream mixture through a sieve, then beat in the vanilla extract and lemon juice. Add the cream, stir well, then process in your ice-cream machine according to the manufacturer's instructions.

Makes about 1 quart

Honey Vanilla

Ingredients

½ cup granulated sugar
6 Tb. honey
¼ cup water
1 large egg, lightly beaten

3 cups well-chilled heavy
 cream
1½ Tb. vanilla extract
dash of salt

Preparation

Place the sugar, honey, and water in a saucepan set over moderate heat and bring to a boil. Stir mixture to dissolve the sugar, then remove from heat and let cool. Add the egg and stir thoroughly.

Place the honey mixture in a large mixing bowl and set that bowl into a larger bowl of ice cubes. Stir briefly, then add 1 cup of cream. Beat with an electric mixer until thickened, about 5 minutes. Add the remaining cream, the vanilla, and the salt, and then blend well.

Transfer the mixture to your ice-cream machine and freeze according to the manufacturer's instructions.

Makes about 1 quart

Variation • Brandy Vanilla

Increase the granulated sugar measure to ¾ cup and eliminate the honey. When adding the chilled cream to the mixture, also add 4 or 5 tablespoons good cognac.

Marshmallow Vanilla

Ingredients

¾ cup marshmallow cream
1 large egg
1 cup half-and-half
¾ cup granulated sugar
1 Tb. vanilla extract
3 cups heavy cream

Preparation

Warm the marshmallow cream in a double boiler. Keep warm. Put the egg, half-and-half, sugar, and vanilla extract in a blender, and blend on medium speed until the mixture is smooth and all the sugar is dissolved. Slowly add the cream and continue blending on low speed until smooth, about 30 seconds. Stir in the warm marshmallow fluff.

Transfer the mixture to your ice-cream machine and freeze according to manufacturer's instructions.

Makes slightly more than 1 quart

Mint Chocolate Chip

Ingredients

1 large egg
1 cup half-and-half
¾ cup granulated sugar
¼ tsp. peppermint oil
   (available from some
   pharmacies)

6 drops green food coloring
   (optional)
3 cups heavy cream
½ to ¾ cup semisweet
   chocolate chips or
   chopped chocolate

Preparation

Put the egg, half-and-half, sugar, peppermint oil, and food coloring in a blender, and blend on medium speed until the mixture is smooth and sugar is dissolved. Slowly add the cream and continue blending on low speed until mixture is smooth, about 30 seconds.

Transfer the mixture to your ice-cream machine and freeze according to manufacturer's instructions. When ice cream is half-frozen, stir in the chocolate chips and continue to freeze.

Makes slightly more than 1 quart

Vanilla Chocolate Chunk

Ingredients

2 to 3 oz. semisweet
  chocolate
1 large egg
1 cup half-and-half

¾ cup granulated sugar
1 Tb. vanilla extract
3 cups heavy cream

Preparation

Chop the chocolate into ¼-inch pieces and chill in the refrigerator. Put the egg, half-and-half, sugar, and vanilla extract in a blender. Blend on medium speed until the mixture is smooth and sugar is dissolved. Slowly add the cream and continue blending on low speed until mixture is smooth, about 30 seconds.

Transfer the mixture to your ice-cream machine and freeze according to manufacturer's instructions. When the ice cream is almost completed, add the chocolate pieces.

Makes slightly more than 1 quart

Variation • Chocolate Flake

2 to 3 oz. bittersweet or semisweet chocolate, preferably in 1 piece

Chill the chocolate in the refrigerator. With a sharp knife, shave the chocolate into flakes. Keep flakes chilled, then add them to the ice cream when it is finished in the machine.

Old-Fashioned Chocolate

Ingredients

3 oz. semisweet chocolate
1 large egg
1 cup half-and-half
¾ cup extrafine sugar
1 tsp. vanilla extract
3 cups heavy cream

Preparation

Chop the chocolate into ¼-inch pieces. Place in a double boiler and melt over hot, but not boiling, water. Keep warm.

Put the egg, half-and-half, sugar, melted chocolate, and vanilla extract in a blender and blend on medium speed until the mixture is smooth and all the sugar is dissolved. Slowly add the cream and continue blending on low speed until smooth, about 30 seconds.

Transfer the mixture to your ice-cream machine, and freeze according to manufacturer's instructions.

Makes slightly more than 1 quart

Opposite: Old-Fashioned Sugar Cones, p. 160.

Chocolate Custard

Ingredients

4 large egg yolks
³/₄ cup granulated sugar
¹/₂ cup half-and-half
1 cup unsweetened cocoa
    powder

2 cups well-chilled heavy
    cream
2 tsp. vanilla extract
¹/₈ tsp. salt

Preparation

Place the egg yolks, sugar, and half-and-half in a large mixing bowl, and beat with an electric hand mixer until foamy and light colored. Stir in the cocoa, adding about ¼ cup at a time until incorporated. Set the bowl over a saucepan filled with hot water and beat until thickened and about double its original volume, about 10 minutes. Remove bowl from heat and place into a larger bowl filled with ice cubes. Beat the mixture until it is no longer warm. Add the cream, vanilla, and salt and continue to beat until quite smooth.

Transfer the mixture to your ice-cream machine and freeze according to the manufacturer's instructions.

Makes about 1 quart

Opposite: Peach Melba Parfait, page 117.

# Chocolate Malted

Ingredients

2 oz. milk chocolate
2 oz. semisweet chocolate
2 Tb. malted milk powder
1 large egg

1 cup half-and-half
¾ cup granulated sugar
2 tsp. vanilla extract
3 cups heavy cream

Preparation

Chop the chocolates into ¼-inch pieces. Place in a double boiler and melt over hot, not boiling, water. Keep warm.

Put the malted milk powder, egg, half-and-half, sugar, and vanilla extract in a blender and blend on medium speed until the mixture is smooth and all the sugar is dissolved. Slowly add the cream, and continue blending on low speed until smooth, about 30 seconds.

Transfer the mixture to your ice-cream machine, and freeze according to manufacturer's instructions.

Makes slightly more than 1 quart

Extra-Bittersweet Chocolate

Ingredients

1 large egg
1 cup half-and-half
¾ cup granulated sugar
1 cup unsweetened cocoa
   powder, preferably
   Callebaut or van Houten

1 tsp. vanilla extract
3 cups heavy cream

Preparation

Put the egg, half-and-half, sugar, cocoa, and vanilla extract in a blender and blend on medium speed until the mixture is smooth and all the sugar is dissolved. Slowly add the cream, and continue blending on low speed until smooth, about 30 seconds.

Transfer the mixture to your ice-cream machine, and freeze according to manufacturer's instructions.

Makes slightly more than 1 quart

Chocolate Cheesecake

Ingredients

1 package (8 oz.) cream
   cheese, at room
   temperature
1 cup granulated sugar
1 cup milk

1 cup unsweetened cocoa
   powder
1 large egg
1 tsp. vanilla extract
2 cups heavy cream

Preparation

Place the cream cheese, sugar, and milk in a blender and whirl at medium speed until smooth, about 1 minute. Add the cocoa and continue to blend until mixture is uniformly dark. Add the egg and vanilla extract. Mix. Slowly add the cream and continue mixing on low speed for about 30 seconds.

Transfer the mixture to your ice-cream machine and freeze according to the manufacturer's instructions.

Makes slightly more than 1 quart

Chocolate Oreo

Ingredients

1 large egg
1 cup half-and-half
¾ cup granulated sugar
1 tsp. vanilla extract

1 cup unsweetened cocoa
  powder
3 cups heavy cream
1 cup broken Oreo cookies

Preparation

Put the egg, half-and-half, sugar, and vanilla extract in a blender and blend on medium speed until the mixture is smooth and all the sugar is dissolved. Slowly add the cocoa while blending at low speed. Blend until smooth. Slowly add the cream and continue blending on low speed until smooth, about 30 seconds. Fold in the cookie pieces.

Transfer the mixture to your ice-cream machine, and freeze according to manufacturer's instructions.

Makes slightly more than 1 quart

Dark Chocolate Almond

Ingredients

4 oz. semisweet chocolate
½ cup blanched almonds
   (not salted)
1 large egg
1 cup half-and-half

¾ cup granulated sugar
1 cup unsweetened cocoa
   powder
1 tsp. vanilla extract
3 cups heavy cream

Preparation

Chop the chocolate into ¼- to ½-inch pieces and melt in a double boiler over hot, but not boiling, water. With a long tweezer, dip an almond into the melted chocolate and coat well. Transfer to a cookie sheet lined with aluminum foil. Repeat for remaining almonds. Chill the chocolate-covered almonds until ready to use.

Put the egg, half-and-half, sugar, cocoa, and vanilla extract in a blender and blend on medium speed until the mixture is smooth and all the sugar is dissolved. Slowly add the cream, and continue blending on low speed until smooth, about 30 seconds.

Transfer the mixture to your ice-cream machine and freeze according to manufacturer's instructions. When the mixture is almost frozen, fold in the almonds and continue freezing until ice cream is the consistency you desire.

Makes slightly more than 1 quart

Variation • Dark Chocolate Raisin

Substitute ½ cup raisins for the blanched almonds. Plump the raisins briefly in hot water, then dry thoroughly before dipping into the melted chocolate.

Chocolate Marzipan Swirl

Ingredients

½ cup marzipan
about ½ cup water
4 oz. semisweet chocolate
1 large egg

1 cup half-and-half
¾ cup granulated sugar
1 tsp. vanilla extract
3 cups heavy cream

Preparation

In a small mixing bowl, place the marzipan and break it up with a spoon. Add water, 1 tablespoon at a time, and blend until marzipan is softened to a thick syrup. Set aside.

Chop the chocolate into ¼-inch pieces. Place in a double boiler and melt over hot, but not boiling, water. Keep warm.

Put the egg, half-and-half, sugar, melted chocolate, and vanilla extract in a blender and blend on medium speed until the mixture is smooth and all the sugar is dissolved. Slowly add the cream and continue blending on low speed until smooth, about 30 seconds.

Transfer the mixture to your ice-cream machine, and freeze according to manufacturer's instructions. When ice cream is almost completed (about the consistency of yogurt), fold in the marzipan but be careful not to blend together. You want to have two separate tastes. Harden in freezer to desired consistency.

Makes slightly more than 1 quart

Chocolate Walnut Brittle

Ingredients

¼ cup unsalted butter
1¼ cups granulated sugar
½ cup chopped walnuts
1 large egg
1 cup half-and-half

1 tsp. vanilla extract
1 cup unsweetened cocoa
   powder
3 cups heavy cream

Preparation

Melt the butter in a saucepan over low heat. Add ½ cup of the sugar and bring to a boil over moderate heat, stirring constantly. Do not allow the mixture to stick to the sides of the pan. Cook until all the sugar is dissolved, and the mixture is light brown in color, about 5 to 7 minutes.

Still over the heat, quickly stir in the chopped walnuts. Pour the mixture onto a lightly greased cookie sheet and spread with the back of a greased spoon. It is important to work quickly, as the walnut brittle cools fast. Let cool, and when hard, break into ½-inch pieces.

Put the egg, half-and-half, remaining sugar, and vanilla extract in a blender and blend on medium speed until the mixture is smooth and all the sugar is dissolved. Slowly add the cocoa while blending at low speed. Blend until smooth. Slowly add the cream and continue blending on low speed until smooth, or for about 30 seconds.

Transfer the mixture to your ice-cream machine, and freeze according to manufacturer's instructions. When mixture is almost frozen, slowly stir in the walnut brittle and continue freezing until the ice cream is the consistency you desire.

Makes slightly more than 1 quart

Chocolate Ginger Chip

Ingredients

6 oz. semisweet chocolate
½ cup chopped crystallized
  ginger
1 large egg

1 cup half-and-half
½ cup granulated sugar
1 tsp. vanilla extract
3 cups heavy cream

Preparation

Chop the chocolate into ½-inch pieces. Place in a double boiler and melt over hot, not boiling, water. With a long tweezers, dip the ginger into the melted chocolate one at a time. Place pieces on a cookie sheet lined with aluminum foil and leaving at least ½-inch space around each. Chill.

Put the egg, half-and-half, sugar, and vanilla extract in a blender and blend on medium speed until the mixture is smooth and sugar is dissolved. Add the melted chocolate and cream, and continue blending on low speed for 30 seconds.

Transfer the mixture to your ice-cream machine and freeze according to manufacturer's instructions. When mixture is almost frozen but still soft, add ginger pieces.

Makes slightly more than 1 quart

Cinnamon Chocolate

Ingredients

1 large egg
1 cup half-and-half
¾ cup granulated sugar
1 tsp. vanilla extract

½ cup unsweetened cocoa
  powder
1 Tb. ground cinnamon
3 cups heavy cream

Preparation

Put the egg, half-and-half, sugar, and vanilla extract in a blender and blend on medium speed until the mixture is smooth and all the sugar is dissolved. Add the chocolate and cinnamon a little at a time while continuing to blend at low speed. Slowly add the cream and blend on low speed for an additional 30 seconds.

Transfer the mixture to your ice-cream machine, and freeze according to the manufacturer's instructions.

Makes slightly more than 1 quart

Mocha Custard

Ingredients

4 oz. milk chocolate
4 large egg yolks
¾ cup extrafine sugar
1 cup half-and-half
1 tsp. vanilla extract

½ cup very strong coffee, or
  1 tsp. instant coffee
  powder
2 cups well-chilled heavy
  cream
dash of salt

Preparation

Break the chocolate into ½-inch pieces and melt in a double boiler over hot, not boiling, water. Keep warm.

In a metal bowl with an electric hand mixer, beat the egg yolks, sugar, half-and-half, and vanilla extract until smooth. Set the bowl over a pan of simmering hot water and beat the mixture until it is thickened and about double its original volume, about 8 minutes. Fold in the melted chocolate and the coffee, and continue beating over hot water until the mixture is smooth, about 2 to 3 minutes.

Set the bowl into a tray of ice cubes and cold water and continue beating until the mixture is cold. Add the cream and salt, and beat well.

40

Transfer the mixture to your ice-cream machine and freeze according to manufacturer's instructions.

Makes about 1 quart

Variations • Mocha Fudge

4 to 6 oz. Chocolate Fudge Sauce (page 189), warmed

When the ice cream has been frozen in the machine, spoon it into a storage container a little at a time, alternating with layers of fudge sauce. Stir once with a large wooden spoon or paddle and allow to harden in freezer until solid.

Mocha Chip

4 to 6 oz. semisweet chocolate chips, or rough ¼-inch chunks of high-quality semisweet chocolate

When the ice cream is almost frozen, stir in the chocolate chips and continue to freeze.

Coffee Custard

Ingredients

4 large egg yolks
¾ cup granulated sugar
1 cup half-and-half
¼ cup instant coffee powder
  (not chunks or crystals)

1 tsp. vanilla extract
2 cups well-chilled heavy
  cream
dash of salt

Preparation

Place the egg yolks, sugar, half-and-half, instant coffee, and vanilla extract in a large mixing bowl, and beat with an electric hand mixer until thickened and about double its original volume, about 10 minutes.

Remove bowl from the heat and immediately place into a larger bowl filled with ice cubes. Beat the mixture steadily until it is no longer warm. Add the cream and salt, and continue to beat until quite smooth. Transfer to your ice-cream machine and freeze according to the manufacturer's directions.

Makes about 1 quart

Opposite: Fruit Bonbons, page 158.
Following page: Uptown Egg Cream, page 137.

Cappuccino

Ingredients

1 large egg
1 cup half-and-half
³/₄ cup granulated sugar
¹/₂ cup espresso (made about
    twice as strong as you
    normally would)

1 tsp. ground cinnamon
1 tsp. vanilla extract
3 cups heavy cream

Preparation

Put the egg, half-and-half, sugar, espresso, cinnamon and vanilla extract in a blender and blend on medium speed until the mixture is smooth and all the sugar is dissolved. Slowly add the cream, and continue blending on low speed for 30 seconds.

Transfer the mixture to your ice-cream machine, and freeze according to manufacturer's instructions.

Makes slightly more than 1 quart

Chestnut Cream

Ingredients

1 cup chestnuts preserved in
  syrup, drained
4 large egg yolks
¾ cup granulated sugar
1 cup half-and-half

1 tsp. vanilla extract
2 cups well-chilled heavy
  cream
dash of salt

Preparation

In a blender or food processor, puree half the chestnuts. Chop the remaining chestnuts into ¼-inch pieces. Set aside.

In a metal bowl with an electric hand mixer, beat the egg yolks, sugar, half-and-half, and vanilla extract. Set the bowl over a saucepan of simmering hot water and beat the mixture until it is thickened and about double its original volume, about 8 minutes. Set the bowl onto a tray of ice cubes and cold water and continue beating until the mixture is cold. Add the heavy cream, salt, and chestnut puree. Beat well, then fold in the chestnut pieces.

Transfer the mixture to your ice-cream machine and freeze according to manufacturer's instructions.

44

Makes about 1 quart

Variation • Chocolate Chestnut

Puree half the chestnuts as described above, and chop the remainder. Make the Chocolate Custard Ice Cream (page 29) and include the pureed chestnuts when you add the heavy cream and salt. Fold in the chestnut pieces, and transfer the mixture to your ice-cream machine. Freeze according to manufacturer's instructions.

Maple Walnut

Ingredients

½ cup pure maple syrup
1 large egg
1 cup half-and-half
½ cup granulated sugar

1 tsp. vanilla extract
3 cups heavy cream
¾ cup chopped walnuts

Preparation

Put the maple syrup, egg, half-and-half, sugar, and vanilla extract in a blender and blend on medium speed until the mixture is smooth and the sugar is dissolved. Slowly add the cream and continue blending on low speed until smooth, about 30 seconds.

Transfer the mixture to your ice-cream machine and freeze according to manufacturer's instructions. When the ice cream is half frozen, add the chopped walnuts.

Makes slightly more than 1 quart

Pistachio

Ingredients

1 large egg
1 cup half-and-half
¾ cup granulated sugar
1 tsp. almond extract
1 tsp. vanilla extract
4 drops green food coloring
   (optional)

3 cups heavy cream
1 cup chopped pistachio
   nuts (unsalted and
   undyed)

Preparation

Put the egg, half-and-half, sugar, almond and vanilla extracts, and food coloring in a blender and blend on medium speed until the mixture is smooth and all the sugar is dissolved. Slowly add the cream and continue blending on low speed for 30 seconds.

Transfer the mixture to your ice-cream machine, and freeze according to manufacturer's instructions. When the ice cream is half frozen, add the chopped nuts.

Makes slightly more than 1 quart

Turkish Delight

Ingredients

1 cup shelled pistachio nuts
  (unsalted and undyed)
1 cup extrafine sugar
1 large egg

1 cup half-and-half
1 tsp. vanilla extract
1 tsp. rosewater
3 cups heavy cream

Preparation

Grind nuts in a food processor fitted with a metal blade for about 30 seconds, or until minced. Add ¼ cup of sugar and continue processing for 10 more seconds. Set aside.

Put the egg, half-and-half, remaining sugar, and vanilla extract in a food processor or blender and blend on medium speed until the mixture is smooth and sugar is dissolved. Add the rosewater and nut-sugar mix, and stir briefly. Slowly add cream and blend on low speed for 30 seconds.

Transfer the mixture to your ice-cream machine, and freeze according to manufacturer's instructions.

Makes slightly more than 1 quart

Tutti-Frutti

Ingredients

1 large egg
1 cup half-and-half
¾ cup extrafine sugar
1 tsp. vanilla extract
2 tsp. almond extract
3 cups heavy cream
½ cup chopped candied
  fruits (¼-inch pieces)

½ cup chopped unsalted
  nuts (almonds,
  macadamias, pistachios,
  and cashews; not peanuts,
  walnuts or brazil nuts)

Preparation

Put the egg, half-and-half, sugar, and extracts in a blender and blend on medium speed until mixture is smooth and sugar is dissolved. Slowly add the cream and continue blending on low speed for 30 seconds. Turn off blender and stir in the fruits and nuts.

Transfer the mixture to your ice-cream machine, and freeze according to manufacturer's instructions.

Makes slightly more than 1 quart

Old-Fashioned Butter Pecan

Ingredients

¼ cup butter
¾ cup chopped pecans
¾ cup dark brown sugar
½ cup half-and-half

1 large egg, lightly beaten
2 cups heavy cream
dash of salt

Preparation

Melt 2 tablespoons of the butter in a skillet and sauté the pecans until lightly browned. Drain on paper towels. Place brown sugar, half-and-half, and remaining butter in a heavy saucepan. Heat over low heat, stirring steadily, until the sugar dissolves and the butter is melted. Let cool.

Place the egg and butter mixture into a blender and blend on medium speed until the mixture is smooth. Slowly add the cream and salt, and continue blending on low speed until mixture is very smooth, about 30 seconds. Add pecans. Transfer the mixture to your ice-cream machine and freeze according to the manufacturer's instructions.

Makes about 1 quart

Butter Pecan Custard

Ingredients

1 cup chopped pecans
¼ cup butter
4 large egg yolks
1 cup half-and-half

¾ cup dark brown sugar
2 cups well-chilled heavy
   cream
dash of salt

Preparation

Melt 2 tablespoons of the butter in a skillet and sauté the pecans until lightly browned. Drain on paper towels. Place the egg yolks in a large mixing bowl, and beat with an electric hand mixer until foamy and light colored. Add the half-and-half and brown sugar. Set the bowl over a saucepan filled with hot water and beat egg and cream mixture until thickened and about double its original volume, about 10 minutes.

Remove bowl from the heat and immediately place into a larger bowl filled with ice cubes. Beat the mixture steadily until it is no longer warm. Add the cream and salt, and continue to beat until quite smooth. Add pecans. Transfer the cream mixture to your ice-cream machine and freeze according to manufacturer's instructions.

Makes about 1 quart

Peanut Butter

Ingredients

¾ cup peanut butter,
   creamy or chunky
¾ cup granulated sugar
2 cups half-and-half

1 large egg
1 Tb. vanilla extract
2 cups heavy cream

Preparation

Place the peanut butter in a double boiler along with the sugar and half the half-and-half. Heat over hot water, stirring frequently, until the peanut butter is soft and has blended with the other ingredients. Continue to heat until the sugar has dissolved. Let cool briefly.

Put the egg, remaining half-and-half, and vanilla in a blender, and blend on medium speed until smooth. Slowly add the peanut butter mixture and blend well. Add the cream and continue on low speed for about 1 minute.

Transfer the mixture to your ice-cream machine and freeze according to the manufacturer's instructions.

Makes slightly more than 1 quart

Variations • Peanut Butter Fudge

3/4 cup Chocolate Fudge Sauce (page 189)

When the peanut butter ice cream is slightly more firm than sour cream, remove it from the ice cream machine and spoon a little into a storage container. Pour on a little of the chocolate fudge sauce—to a layer about ⅛ to ¼ inch thick. Add another layer of ice cream and another layer of fudge sauce and continue until you've added all the sauce and ice cream. Stir once with a wooden spoon, pulling the spoon out as you turn it. Place in freezer to harden.

Peanut Butter Chocolate Chip

When the peanut butter ice cream is semi-firm, stir in ½ cup chopped chocolate pieces and continue to freeze.

# Hazelnut

Ingredients

1 cup chopped hazelnuts
1 large egg
1 cup half-and-half
¾ cup granulated sugar

1 tsp. vanilla extract
3 cups heavy cream
1 Tb. hazelnut liqueur
   (optional)

Preparation

Preheat the oven to 350°.

Spread the nuts on a cookie sheet or in a shallow pan and toast in oven for about 10 minutes. Grind nuts in a food processor for about 1 minute, or until the nuts form a smooth paste.

Put the egg, nut paste, half-and-half, sugar, and vanilla extract into the bowl of a food processor or into a blender. Blend on medium speed until the mixture is smooth and all the sugar is dissolved. Slowly add the heavy cream and liqueur, if using, and continue blending on low speed until smooth, about 30 seconds.

Transfer the mixture to your ice-cream machine, and freeze according to the manufacturer's instructions.

Makes slightly more than 1 quart

Variation • Chocolate Hazelnut

Add ½ cup unsweetened cocoa powder to the egg, nut paste, half-and-half, sugar, and vanilla in the food processor or blender and blend until smooth.

Dutch Apple

Ingredients

2 ripe tart apples, such as Granny Smiths or Jonathans
3 Tb. ground cinnamon
¾ cup extrafine sugar
¼ cup water

1 large egg
1 cup half-and-half
1 Tb. vanilla extract
3 cups heavy cream

Preparation

Peel and core the apples. Cut them into ¼-inch dice and put them in a saucepan, along with the cinnamon, half the sugar, and the water. Cook the mixture over low heat for about 10 to 15 minutes, or until apples are soft. Chill.

Put the egg, half-and-half, remaining sugar, and vanilla extract in a blender and blend on medium speed until the mixture is smooth and all the sugar is dissolved. Slowly add the cream and continue blending on low speed for 30 seconds.

Transfer the mixture to your ice-cream machine and freeze according to the manufacturer's instructions. When the ice cream is about half frozen, add the apple-cinnamon mixture and continue freezing.

56

Makes slightly more than 1 quart

Variation • Apple Jack Raisin

Soak ½ cup dark raisins in ⅓ cup apple brandy until they have swelled. Add the raisins, along with any remaining liquid, just before you transfer the mixture to your ice-cream machine.

 *Apricot*

Ingredients

³/₄ cup dried apricots
¹/₄ cup cognac
¹/₄ cup water
1 large egg

1 cup half-and-half
³/₄ cup granulated sugar
1 tsp. vanilla extract
3 cups heavy cream

Preparation

Cut the apricots into ¼-inch pieces and place them in a saucepan over low heat. Add the cognac and the water and simmer, uncovered, for 10 minutes, or until the apricots swell. Remove from the heat and chill in the refrigerator.

Put the egg, half-and-half, sugar, and vanilla extract in a blender and blend on medium speed until the mixture is smooth and the sugar is dissolved. Add the apricot mixture and blend again, then add the cream slowly and continue blending on low speed for an additional 30 seconds.

Transfer the mixture to your ice-cream machine and freeze according to the manufacturer's instructions.

Makes slightly more than 1 quart

Variation • Apricot Almond

When the mixture is half-frozen, stir in ½ cup chopped blanched almonds and continue to freeze.

Opposite: Chocolate Mint Bombe, page 156.

Cantaloupe

Ingredients

½ ripe medium-size
   cantaloupe
2 tsp. lemon juice
¾ cup granulated sugar
1 large egg

1 cup half-and-half
1 tsp. vanilla extract
3 cups heavy cream

Preparation

Cut the rind off the cantaloupe, and clean the seeds from the center. Cut the pulp into ½-inch pieces and then put the pieces into a blender or food processor. Add the lemon juice. Puree for about 1 minute, then add the sugar and process for another 30 seconds or until all the sugar is dissolved. Pour mixture into a bowl and set aside.

Put the egg, half-and-half, and vanilla extract into the blender or processor and blend on medium speed until the mixture is smooth. Add the cantaloupe puree and blend. Slowly add the cream and continue blending on low speed for an additional 30 seconds.

Transfer the mixture to your ice-cream machine and freeze according to manufacturer's instructions.

Makes slightly more than 1 quart

Opposite: Fried Ice Cream, page 165.

Banana Fudge Swirl

Ingredients

3 large, ripe bananas
1½ Tb. lemon juice
¾ cup granulated sugar
1 large egg
1 cup half-and-half

1 Tb. vanilla extract or
   banana liqueur
3 cups heavy cream
1 cup Chocolate Fudge
   Sauce (page 189)

Preparation

Peel the bananas and remove areas that are very overripe. Cut into ½-inch slices. Put bananas, along with lemon juice, in a blender or food processor and puree for about 1½ minutes. Add ½ cup sugar and process until sugar is dissolved. Place in bowl and set aside.

Put the egg, half-and-half, remaining sugar, and vanilla extract in a blender and blend on medium speed until the mixture is smooth. Add the banana puree, briefly spin again, then slowly add the cream. Continue blending on low speed for 30 seconds.

Transfer the mixture to your ice-cream machine, and freeze according to the manufacturer's instructions. After ice cream is finished in the machine, spoon a 1-inch layer into the bottom of your freezer container. Add a ½-inch layer of chocolate fudge sauce, then follow with another layer of ice cream. Repeat until you have filled the container with the ice cream and the sauce. Using a wooden spoon, stir the mixture once, pulling the spoon out as you turn it. Place container in freezer to harden.

Makes slightly more than 1 quart

Variation • Banana Chocolate Chip

Proceed with recipe as indicated for swirl, but omit the chocolate fudge sauce. Instead, fold in ¾ cup chopped semisweet chocolate after the ice cream is half-frozen.

Banana Rum Custard

Ingredients

3 large, ripe bananas
2½ Tb. lemon juice
2 Tb. dark rum, preferably
   Myer's
1 cup extrafine sugar
4 large egg yolks

1 cup half-and-half
1 Tb. vanilla extract
2 cups well-chilled heavy
   cream
dash of salt

Preparation

Peel the bananas and remove any areas that are very overripe. Cut into ½-inch slices. Put them, along with the lemon juice and the rum, into a food processor or blender and puree for about 1½ minutes. Add ½ cup sugar and process until sugar is dissolved. Set aside.

In a metal bowl, with an electric hand mixer, beat the egg yolks, remaining sugar, half-and-half, and vanilla extract. Set the bowl over a pan of hot water and continue to beat the mixture until it is thickened and about double its original volume, about 10 minutes. Add the banana puree and beat until smooth, another minute.

Set the bowl into a tray of ice cubes and continue beating until the mixture is cold. Add the cream and salt and beat mixture for an additional minute, until smooth.

Transfer the mixture to your ice-cream machine, and freeze according to manufacturer's instructions.

Makes about 1 quart

Fresh Blackberry

Ingredients

1 pt. fresh, ripe blackberries
1 cup granulated sugar
1 large egg
1 tsp. lemon juice
1 cup half-and-half

1 tsp. vanilla extract
3 to 4 Tb. crème de cassis
  (optional)
3 cups heavy cream

Preparation

Place blackberries in a double boiler and add ½ cup of the sugar. Stir to mix well, then place saucepan over low heat to soften the berries and release juice, about 10 minutes.

When softened, transfer the berry mixture to a blender and spin for 1 minute, or until pureed. You can strain out the seeds with a fine sieve, though I prefer not to. Transfer the puree to a bowl and place in the refrigerator until cool.

Put the egg, lemon juice, half-and-half, remaining sugar, vanilla extract, and liqueur, if using, in the blender and blend on medium speed until the mixture is smooth and all the sugar is dissolved. Slowly add the cream and continue blending on low speed for about 30 seconds.

Transfer the mixture to your ice-cream machine and freeze according to the manufacturer's instructions. When the ice cream is about half-frozen, slowly add the blackberry puree and continue freezing.

Makes slightly more than 1 quart

Sweet Cherry

Ingredients

1½ cups pitted ripe sweet
   cherries
1 cup granulated sugar
¼ cup water

1 large egg
1 cup half-and-half
1 tsp. vanilla extract
3 cups heavy cream

Preparation

Place the cherries in a double boiler with about half the sugar and the water. Heat for about 10 minutes to allow the fruit to soften and release its juices. Transfer mixture to a blender and puree. Place puree in a bowl and chill.

Put the egg, half-and-half, remaining sugar, vanilla extract and cherry puree in blender. Blend on medium speed until the mixture is smooth and sugar is dissolved. Slowly add cream and blend for 30 seconds.

Transfer mixture to your ice-cream machine and freeze according to manufacturer's instructions.

Makes slightly more than 1 quart

Variation • Cherry Vanilla

Instead of putting the cherries in the double boiler, just place them in a bowl with ¼ cup sugar (no water) and let sit for about 2 hours. Drain; do not puree.

Place the egg, half-and-half, ¾ cup sugar, and vanilla extract in a blender and blend on medium speed until the mixture is smooth and sugar is dissolved. As directed, add the cream, blend, and then transfer to ice-cream machine. When the ice cream is almost frozen but still turning in the canister, add the cherries and continue to process until frozen.

Coconut Custard

Ingredients

4 large egg yolks
¾ cup extrafine sugar
1 cup half-and-half
1 tsp. vanilla extract
½ cup coconut cream

2 cups well-chilled heavy
   cream
dash of salt
¼ cup sweetened shredded
   coconut

Preparation

In a metal bowl, with an electric hand mixer, beat the egg yolks, sugar, half-and-half, and vanilla extract. Set the bowl over a pan of hot water and beat the mixture until it is thickened and about double its original volume, about 10 minutes. Beat in the coconut cream. Place the bowl in a tray of ice cubes and continue beating until the mixture is cold. Add the cream and salt, and beat the mixture well. Fold in the coconut.

Transfer the mixture to your ice-cream machine, and freeze according to the manufacturer's instructions.

Makes about 1 quart

Spiced Cranberry

Ingredients

1 cup fresh cranberries
½ cup brown sugar
¾ cup apple cider
1 large egg
1 cup half-and-half

¾ cup granulated sugar
1 tsp. vanilla extract
¼ tsp. each ground cloves,
   allspice, cinnamon
3 cups heavy cream

Preparation

In an enamel saucepan, cook the cranberries in the brown sugar and cider until they pop. Remove berries and reserve. Measure ¼ cup liquid and chill both.

Put cooking liquid, egg, half-and-half, sugar, extract, and spices in a blender and blend on medium until mixture is smooth and sugar is dissolved. Add cream slowly and blend on low speed for 30 seconds.

Transfer mixture to an ice-cream machine and freeze according to instructions. When ice cream is half-frozen, add cranberries.

Makes slightly more than 1 quart

Kiwi Custard

Ingredients

5 ripe, fresh kiwifruit
1 cup extrafine sugar
4 large egg yolks
1 cup half-and-half

1 Tb. vanilla extract
2 cups well-chilled heavy
  cream
dash of salt

Preparation

Peel the kiwifruit and cut into ¼-inch pieces. Mix the kiwi pieces with ½ cup of the sugar and allow to macerate for 2 to 3 hours. Chill in the refrigerator.

In a metal bowl, with an electric hand mixer, beat the egg yolks, remaining sugar, half-and-half, and vanilla extract. Set the bowl over a pan of hot water and beat the mixture until thickened and double its original volume, about 10 minutes.

Place the bowl in a tray of ice cubes and continue beating until the mixture is cold. Add the cream and salt, and beat the mixture well.

Transfer the mixture to your ice-cream machine, and freeze it according to the manufacturer's instructions. When mixture is half-frozen, add kiwifruit and continue to freeze.

Makes about 1 quart

Lemon Custard

Ingredients

3 large, ripe lemons
¾ cup extrafine sugar
4 large egg yolks
1 cup half-and-half

1 Tb. vanilla extract
2 cups well-chilled heavy
  cream
dash of salt

Preparation

Remove the zest from the lemons and combine it with the sugar in a food processor fitted with a metal blade. Grind for about 3 to 4 minutes, or until the zest and the sugar are finely ground and mixed. Squeeze about 2 tablespoons of the juice from the lemons and mix this into the lemon sugar.

In a metal bowl, with an electric hand mixer, beat the egg yolks, lemon sugar, half-and-half, and vanilla extract. Set the bowl in a pan of hot water and beat the mixture until thickened and doubled, about 10 minutes.

Place the bowl in a tray of ice cubes, and continue beating until the mixture is cold. Add the cream and salt and beat the mixture well.

Transfer the mixture to your ice-cream freezer, and freeze it according to the manufacturer's instructions.

Makes about 1 quart

Mandarin Orange Coconut

Ingredients

1 can mandarin orange
   slices, well drained
¼ cup sweetened shredded
   coconut
2 Tb. coconut cream

1 large egg
1 cup half-and-half
¾ cup granulated sugar
1 tsp. vanilla extract
3 cups heavy cream

Preparation

Put the oranges, coconut, and coconut cream in a blender or food processor and puree for about 1 minute. Transfer to a bowl and set aside.

Put the egg, half-and-half, sugar, and vanilla extract in the blender and blend on medium speed until the mixture is smooth and sugar is dissolved. Slowly add the cream and blend on low speed for 30 seconds more.

Transfer the mixture to your ice-cream machine, and freeze according to manufacturer's instructions. When ice cream is about half-frozen, slowly stir in the orange-coconut puree. Continue to freeze.

Makes slightly more than 1 quart

Variation • Orange Chocolate Chip

Proceed as above but omit shredded coconut and coconut cream. When ice cream is half-frozen, fold in ¾ cup semi-sweet chocolate chip morsels.

Mango

Ingredients

2 or 3 large, ripe mangoes,
 slightly soft
¾ cup granulated sugar
1 large egg

1 cup half-and-half
1 tsp. vanilla extract
3 cups heavy cream

Preparation

With a sharp knife, remove the skin from the mangoes, taking care not to remove any of the flesh. Cut as much of the flesh off the pit as you can, then cut into ¼- to ½-inch pieces. Combine the mango pieces with half the sugar in a double boiler and cook over hot water for 10 to 15 minutes to soften the fruit and release the juices. Transfer mixture to a blender and puree. Put mango puree into a bowl and chill.

Put the egg, half-and-half, remaining sugar, and vanilla extract in a blender and blend on medium speed until the mixture is smooth and the sugar is dissolved. Add the mango puree and briefly spin. Slowly add the cream and continue blending on low speed for 30 seconds more. Transfer the mixture to your ice-cream machine and freeze according to instructions.

Makes slightly more than 1 quart

Opposite: Butterscotch Marshmallow Sundae, page 102.
Following page: Chocolate Gingerbread Ice Cream Roll, page 182.

Marmalade

Ingredients

¾ cup imported English
   marmalade, preferably
   Chivers (tart flavor with
   pieces of rind)
¼ cup water
1 large egg

1 cup half-and-half
¼ cup granulated sugar
1 tsp. vanilla extract
3 cups heavy cream

Preparation

Put the marmalade with the water into a double boiler and heat until melted. Place in a blender along with the egg, half-and-half, sugar, and vanilla extract. Blend on medium speed until the sugar is dissolved. There will still be some chunks of rind in the mixture. Slowly add the cream and continue blending on low speed until smooth, about 30 seconds.

Transfer the mixture to your ice-cream machine and freeze according to manufacturer's instructions.

Makes slightly more than 1 quart

Opposite: Pousse Café Parfait, page 118.
Preceding page: Ice Cream Almond Fritters with Melba Sauce, page 166.

Buttermilk Peach

Ingredients

1 pt. fresh, ripe peaches
¾ cup buttermilk
1 large egg
1 cup half-and-half

¾ cup extrafine sugar
1 tsp. vanilla extract
¼ tsp. almond extract
3 cups heavy cream

Preparation

Blanch the peaches in boiling water for 30 seconds, then cool, peel, and discard pits. Cut into ¼- to ½-inch pieces. Place peaches, buttermilk, egg, half-and-half, sugar, and vanilla extract in a blender and blend on medium speed until mixture is smooth and sugar is dissolved. Slowly add cream and blend on low speed for 30 seconds.

Transfer the mixture to your ice-cream freezer and freeze according to manufacturer's instructions.

Makes slightly more than 1 quart

76

# Amaretto Peach

Ingredients

1½ to 2 lb. ripe peaches
1 cup granulated sugar
1 large egg
1 cup half-and-half

1 tsp. vanilla extract
1 Tb. amaretto liqueur
3 cups heavy cream

Preparation

Blanch the peaches in boiling water for 30 seconds. Cool under cold running water; peel, then remove pits. Cut peaches into ¼-inch pieces. Mix with ½ cup of sugar and heat in a double boiler for 10 to 15 minutes, stirring occasionally, until fruit is soft. Place in mixing bowl and let cool.

Put the egg, half-and-half, remaining sugar, vanilla extract, and amaretto into a blender and blend on medium speed until the mixture is smooth and sugar is dissolved. Slowly add the cream and blend on low speed for 30 seconds more.

Transfer the mixture to your ice-cream machine and freeze according to manufacturer's instructions. When ice cream is half-frozen, fold in the peaches and continue processing.

Makes slightly more than 1 quart

Pear

Ingredients

juice of 1 lemon
¼ cup water
3 ripe pears (Anjou,
   Bartletts)
¾ cup granulated sugar
1 large egg

1 cup half-and-half
2 Tb. pear eau-de-vie
3 cups heavy cream

Preparation

Combine the lemon juice with the water in an enamel saucepan. Halve the pears, peel them, and remove cores. Cut pears into ½-inch pieces, then add them and half the sugar to the lemon water. Bring to a boil, cover, and let simmer for 10 minutes, or until pears are very soft. Transfer mixture to a blender or food processor and puree for 1 minute. Transfer puree to a mixing bowl and let cool in refrigerator.

Put the egg, half-and-half, remaining sugar, and *eau-de-vie* in a blender and blend on medium speed until the mixture is smooth. Slowly add the cream and blend on low speed for 30 seconds. Stir in the reserved pear puree.

Transfer the mixture to your ice-cream machine, and freeze according to manufacturer's instructions.

Makes slightly more than 1 quart

Variation • Pear Fudge

1 cup Chocolate Fudge Sauce (page 189)

Prepare the Pear Ice Cream as directed and freeze to the consistency of sour cream (or slightly harder). Spoon the mixture out of the machine container and place about a 1-inch layer into your freezer container. Cover the ice cream with a thin (⅛-inch) layer of fudge sauce. Add another layer of ice cream about 1 inch thick, then another layer of fudge sauce. Continue until all the fudge sauce and all the ice cream are in the container. Stir once with a wooden spoon, pulling the spoon out as you turn. Place in the freezer to harden.

Pumpkin Pie

Ingredients

1 small pumpkin, ¹/₂ to
  ³/₄ lb.
³/₄ cup brown sugar
¹/₄ cup water
¹/₄ tsp. each ground ginger,
  nutmeg, allspice, cloves
4 large egg yolks

³/₄ cup extrafine sugar
1 cup half-and-half
1 tsp. vanilla extract
2 cups well-chilled heavy
  cream
dash of salt

Preparation

Cut the pumpkin in half and remove the seeds and membranes in the center. Remove the skin, and cut the flesh into ¹/₂-inch pieces. Place pumpkin in a saucepan along with the brown sugar and water. Bring to a boil, cover, and let simmer, stirring occasionally, for 10 to 15 minutes or until the pumpkin is quite tender. Drain and mash the pumpkin. Season the puree with the spices and then chill in refrigerator.

In a metal bowl, with an electric hand mixer, beat the egg yolks, sugar, half-and-half, and vanilla extract. Set the bowl in a pan of hot water and beat the mixture until it is thickened and about double its original volume, about 10 minutes.

Set the bowl into a tray of ice cubes, and continue beating until the mixture is cold. Add the cream and salt, and beat the mixture well. Fold in the mashed pumpkin.

Transfer the mixture to your ice-cream machine, and freeze it according to manufacturer's instructions.

Makes about 1 quart

 # Red Plum

Ingredients

1½ to 2 lb. ripe red plums
1 cup granulated sugar
1 large egg

1 cup half-and-half
1 tsp. vanilla extract
3 cups heavy cream

Preparation

Blanch the plums for 30 seconds in boiling water, cool in cold water, then remove the skins. Cut the plums into ¼-inch pieces, removing the pits. Place plums in a double boiler and add ½ cup of the sugar. Mix thoroughly then heat the plum-sugar mixture for 10 to 15 minutes, stirring occasionally. Let cool in the refrigerator. Put the egg, half-and-half, remaining sugar, and vanilla extract in a blender and blend on medium speed until the mixture is smooth and the sugar is dissolved. Slowly add the cream and blend on low speed for 30 seconds more.

Transfer the mixture to your ice-cream machine, and freeze according to the manufacturer's instructions. When the ice cream is about half-frozen, fold in the chilled plum mixture and continue to freeze.

Makes slightly more than 1 quart

Variation • Brandied Plum Raisin

Soak ½ cup raisins in ⅓ cup brandy. Follow recipe as indicated, and fold in raisins and any remaining liquid just before placing mixture into ice-cream freezer. Freeze as directed.

Fresh Raspberry

Ingredients

1 pt. fresh raspberries
1¼ cups extrafine sugar
1 large egg
1 cup half-and-half

1 tsp. vanilla extract or
   raspberry liqueur
3 cups heavy cream

Preparation

Sort through raspberries and place in a double boiler. Add ½ cup sugar and heat for 10 to 15 minutes, or until fruit is soft. Transfer to a blender and spin until a puree. You can strain the seeds out of the puree; I prefer not to. Transfer to a bowl and let cool in refrigerator.

Put the egg, half-and-half, remaining sugar, and vanilla extract or liqueur in a blender and blend on medium speed until the mixture is smooth and the sugar is dissolved. Slowly add the cream and continue blending on low speed for 30 seconds.

Transfer the mixture to your ice-cream machine, and freeze according to manufacturer's instructions. When the ice cream is about half-frozen, slowly add the raspberry puree to the mixture. Continue freezing.

Makes slightly more than 1 quart

Old-Fashioned Strawberry

Ingredients

1 pt. strawberries
1 cup granulated sugar
1 large egg

1 cup half-and-half
1 tsp. vanilla extract
3 cups heavy cream

Preparation

Hull the strawberries and cut the larger ones in half. Place the berries in a double boiler and add ½ cup sugar. Heat for 10 to 15 minutes, stirring occasionally, until the fruit is very soft. Puree the fruit in a blender. You can strain the seeds out of the puree, but I prefer not to. Transfer puree to a bowl and cool in the refrigerator.

Put the egg, half-and-half, remaining sugar, and vanilla extract in a blender and blend on medium speed until the mixture is smooth and the sugar is dissolved. Slowly add the cream and continue blending on low speed for 30 seconds.

Transfer the mixture to your ice-cream freezer, and freeze according to manufacturer's instructions. When the ice cream is about half-frozen, add the strawberry puree to the mixture. Continue freezing.

Makes slightly more than 1 quart

Rum Raisin

Ingredients

½ cup raisins
¾ cup dark rum, preferably
 Myer's
1 large egg
1 cup half-and-half

¾ cup granulated sugar
1 Tb. vanilla extract
3 cups heavy cream

Preparation

Put the raisins and rum into a double boiler and heat them for 10 minutes, uncovered, until raisins swell. Drain raisins and set aside. Pour the rum liquid into a blender and add the egg, half-and-half, sugar, and vanilla extract. Blend on medium speed until the mixture is smooth and the sugar is dissolved. Slowly add the cream and blend on low speed for 30 seconds more.

Transfer the mixture to your ice-cream machine and freeze according to the manufacturer's instructions. When the ice cream is about half-frozen, add the raisins and continue processing.

Makes slightly more than 1 quart

Cinnamon

Ingredients

1 large egg
1 cup half-and-half
¾ cup granulated sugar

5 tsp. ground cinnamon
1 Tb. vanilla extract
3 cups heavy cream

Preparation

Put the egg, half-and-half, sugar, cinnamon, and vanilla extract in a blender and blend on medium speed until the mixture is smooth and the sugar is dissolved. Slowly add the cream and blend on low speed for 30 seconds more.

Transfer the mixture to your ice-cream machine, and freeze according to the manufacturer's instructions.

Makes slightly more than 1 quart

# *Fresh Ginger*

Ingredients

⅓ cup peeled and diced
   fresh ginger
½ cup brown sugar
½ cup water
1 large egg

1 cup half-and-half
¾ cup extrafine sugar
3 cups heavy cream

Preparation

Boil the ginger in a saucepan with the brown sugar and water for about 20 minutes, or until ginger is soft. Drain, discarding the liquid. Chill ginger.

Put the ginger, egg, half-and-half, and sugar in a blender and blend on medium speed until the mixture is smooth and the sugar is dissolved. Slowly add the cream and blend on low speed for 30 seconds more.

Transfer the mixture to your ice-cream machine and freeze according to manufacturer's instructions.

Makes slightly more than 1 quart

Eggnog

Ingredients

4 large egg yolks
¾ cup extrafine sugar
1 cup half-and-half
1 tsp. ground nutmeg
1 tsp. vanilla extract

3 Tb. bourbon
3 Tb. cognac
2 cups well-chilled heavy
  cream
dash of salt

Preparation

In a metal bowl, with an electric hand mixer, beat the egg yolks, sugar, half-and-half, nutmeg, and vanilla extract. Set the bowl in a pan of hot water and beat the mixture until it is thickened and about double its original volume, about 10 minutes. Stir in the bourbon and cognac. Set the bowl into a tray of ice cubes, and continue beating until the mixture is cold. Add the cream and salt and beat the mixture well.

Transfer the mixture to your ice-cream machine and freeze it according to manufacturer's instructions.

Makes about 1 quart

Peppermint

Ingredients

½ cup finely crushed
   peppermint candy or ¼
   tsp. peppermint oil
¼ cup crème de menthe
1 large egg
1 cup half-and-half

½ cup granulated sugar
1 tsp. vanilla extract
3 cups heavy cream
4 drops red food coloring
   (optional)

Preparation

Put the crushed peppermint candy and the crème de menthe in a blender and blend on high speed for about 30 seconds. Add the egg, half and half, sugar, and vanilla extract, and blend on medium speed until the mixture is smooth and the sugar is dissolved. Slowly add the cream and blend on low speed for 30 seconds.

Transfer the mixture to your ice-cream machine and freeze according to manufacturer's instructions.

Makes slightly more than 1 quart

Opposite: Cherry Almond Sundae, page 104.

Anisette

Ingredients

½ cup finely crushed hard
  licorice candy
¼ cup anisette liqueur
1 large egg
1 cup half-and-half

¾ cup granulated sugar
1 Tb. vanilla extract
3 cups heavy cream

Preparation

Put the licorice candy and the anisette in a blender and blend on high speed for about 30 seconds. Add the egg, half-and-half, sugar, and vanilla extract and blend on medium speed until the mixture is smooth and the sugar is dissolved. Slowly add the cream and blend on low speed for 30 seconds.

Transfer the mixture to your ice-cream machine and freeze according to manufacturer's instructions.

Makes slightly more than 1 quart

Opposite: Mint Julep Slush, page 142.

Green Tea

Ingredients

¼ cup very strong brewed
green tea (4 times regular
strength)
1 large egg

1 cup half-and-half
¾ cup granulated sugar
3 cups heavy cream

Preparation

Put the green tea, egg, half-and-half, and sugar in a blender and blend on medium speed until the mixture is smooth and the sugar is dissolved. Slowly add the cream and blend on low speed for 30 minutes.

Transfer the mixture to your ice-cream machine and freeze according to manufacturer's instructions.

Makes slightly more than 1 quart

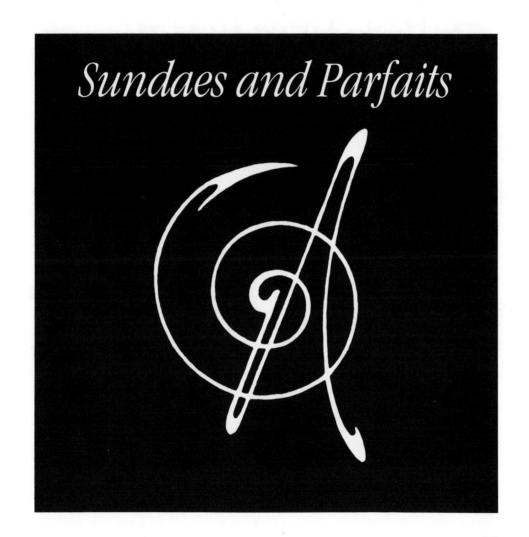

Sundaes and Parfaits

Apple Spice Parfait

Ingredients

¼ cup Cinnamon Sauce
2 scoops Dutch Apple Ice
  Cream
3 Tb. crumbs from a spice
  cake or other dark,
  crumbly cake
¼ cup whipped cream

Preparation

Place a tablespoon of sauce at the bottom of a parfait glass. Add a scoop of ice cream, then sprinkle ice cream with a tablespoon of cake crumbs. Layer on another scoop of ice cream, pour on some more sauce, and sprinkle top with more cake crumbs. Garnish with a swirl of whipped cream and a dusting of cake crumbs.

Makes 1 serving

Apple Toddy

Ingredients

1 medium-size baking apple
1 tsp. ground cinnamon
2 Tb. granulated sugar

1 scoop Vanilla or
   Cinnamon Ice Cream
3 Tb. calvados
pinch of nutmeg

Preparation

Preheat the oven to 325°.

Core and peel the apple. Mix the cinnamon and sugar, and cover the peeled apple with it, placing any extra cinnamon sugar in the center of the apple. Bake the apple for 30 minutes, then remove from oven and put on a dessert plate.

While still hot, place the scoop of ice cream in the center of the apple. Drizzle on the calvados and garnish with nutmeg. Serve while the apple is still quite warm.

Makes 1 serving

Baklava Parfait

Ingredients

¹/₂ cup honey
1 cup chopped pistachio
    nuts (not dyed or salted)
8 scoops Pistachio Ice
    Cream
ground cinnamon

Preparation

Place 1 tablespoon honey in each of 4 parfait glasses and sprinkle in a small amount of the pistachios.

Put 1 scoop of the ice cream in each glass. Drizzle on 1 more tablespoon of the honey. Add more pistachios and sprinkle with cinnamon. Put a second scoop of the ice cream in each glass. Divide the remaining pistachio nuts among the 4 glasses, drizzle on more honey. Sprinkle tops with cinnamon. Garnish with a plain wafer cookie or a cinnamon stick, if desired.

Makes 4 parfaits

Photo 3 following page 106

Banana Ginger Parfait

Ingredients

4 scoops Banana Custard
    Ice Cream
½ cup Ginger Sauce
2 Tb. chopped crystallized
    ginger
1 ripe banana, peeled and
    sliced

Preparation

Place a scoop of ice cream into the bottoms of 2 parfait glasses. Spoon on a little ginger sauce, then sprinkle with a few pieces of chopped ginger. Add another scoop of ice cream. Divide the banana slices between the 2 glasses, and spoon on more sauce. Top with a few pieces of ginger.

Makes 2 parfaits

Banana Split

Ingredients

1 ripe banana
1 scoop Chocolate Ice Cream
1 scoop Vanilla Ice Cream
1 scoop Cherry Vanilla Ice Cream
¼ cup Pineapple Topping

¼ cup Strawberry Topping
¼ cup Chocolate Sauce
½ cup whipped cream
¼ cup chopped mixed nuts or shredded coconut
maraschino cherries with stems

Preparation

Peel the banana and split it lengthwise. Place it in a long dish, preferably with high sides (sometimes called a banana split dish). Put 1 scoop each of the 3 ice creams into the dish. Pour or spoon the toppings on in layers so that each flavor of ice cream gets a topping.

Add the whipped cream and sprinkle with the chopped nuts or coconut. Garnish with cherries.

Makes 1 split

Photo 1 following page 106

Black Berry Sundae

Ingredients

2 Tb. blackberry brandy
1 Tb. granulated sugar
½ cup fresh blackberries
1 scoop Fresh Raspberry Ice
   Cream

Preparation

In a small bowl, mix the brandy with the sugar until dissolved. Add the berries and let macerate for at least 30 minutes.

Place the ice cream in a serving dish and top with the blackberry mixture.

Makes 1 sundae

Photo 4 following page 138

Black-Out Sundae

Ingredients

2 oz. bittersweet or
  semisweet chocolate,
  chilled
1 or 2 scoops
  Extra-Bittersweet
  Chocolate Ice Cream

½ cup Hot Fudge Sauce
whipped cream

Preparation

Scrape off small shavings from the chocolate and place on a piece of waxed paper or in a dish.

Roll the scoop of ice cream in the chocolate shavings and then place ice cream in a sherbet cup or similar serving dish. Pour on the sauce and garnish with whipped cream.

Makes 1 sundae

Brandied Peach Sundae

Ingredients

2 small, ripe freestone
   peaches
¼ cup brandy
2 large scoops Vanilla
   Custard Ice Cream

2 Tb. grenadine
whipped cream
chopped walnuts or
   almonds

Preparation

Peel and halve the peaches, then remove the pits. Slice the peaches into ½-inch sections and mix in a bowl with the brandy. Let sit for about 30 minutes.

Place a large scoop of ice cream into each of 2 dessert dishes. Add the grenadine to each, then pour over the peach and brandy mixture. Top with a dollop of whipped cream and sprinkle with nuts.

Makes 2 sundaes

Butterscotch Marshmallow Sundae

Ingredients

2 scoops Vanilla Custard Ice
  Cream
½ cup Butterscotch Sauce

½ cup Marshmallow
  Topping

Preparation

Place ice cream in a large dessert dish and pour on sauce.
Spoon topping over and serve immediately.

Makes 1 serving

Photo 1 following page 74

Cappuccino Sundae

Ingredients

4 scoops Cappuccino or
   Coffee Custard Ice Cream
$^1/_2$ cup Cinnamon Sauce

$^1/_2$ cup Coffee Sauce
whipped cream

Preparation

Place 1 scoop of ice cream into each of 4 sundae dishes. Pour sauces over each and top with a dollop of whipped cream. Serve immediately, with almond macaroons.

Makes 4 sundaes

Cherry Almond Sundae

Ingredients

4 scoops Cherry Vanilla or
   Vanilla Custard Ice
   Cream
1 cup Cherry Sauce
¼ cup brandy
1 can (14 oz.) whole pitted
   canned sweet cherries,
   drained

1 cup sliced blanched
   almonds
1 cup whipped cream

Preparation

Place 1 scoop of ice cream in each of 4 sundae dishes. Top
each with ¼ cup of the sauce. Pour 1 tablespoon brandy over
each, then distribute the cherries among the dishes. Scatter
on the almonds and top each with a large swirl of whipped
cream.

Makes 4 sundaes

Photo 1 following page 90

Chestnut Parfait

Ingredients

4 scoops Vanilla Malted Ice
 Cream
$^1/_2$ cup Chestnut Sauce

$^1/_2$ cup drained and chopped
 chestnuts preserved in
 syrup

Preparation

Place 1 scoop of ice cream in each of 2 parfait glasses. Add about 1 tablespoon of sauce to each, then add another scoop of ice cream. Top with chestnut pieces and pour remaining sauce overall.

Makes 2 parfaits

Chocolate Raspberry Reward

Ingredients

2 cups fresh raspberries
1/4 cup granulated sugar
1/2 cup framboise liqueur
1 oz. semisweet chocolate, chilled

4 scoops Chocolate Ice Cream
1/4 cup whipped cream

Preparation

Place the raspberries in a saucepan with the sugar and liqueur, and simmer gently for 5 to 7 minutes. Remove the raspberries from the pan with a slotted spoon and set aside. Let both fruit and liquid cool. Scrape shavings from the chocolate and set aside. Keep cold.

Distribute half the raspberry liquid among 4 parfait glasses. Add a scoop of ice cream to each glass. Scatter the raspberries among the glasses and then pour on remaining liquid. Top with chocolate shavings, and garnish with whipped cream.

Makes 4 parfaits

Opposite: Banana Split, page 98.
Following page: Vanilla, Strawberry, and Chocolate Malted, pages 130-131.

Dusty Road Parfait

Ingredients

4 scoops Vanilla Fudge Ice
    Cream
$1/2$ cup Caramel Sauce

$1/4$ cup crushed malted milk
    balls

Preparation

Place a scoop of ice cream into each of 2 parfait glasses. Pour 1 tablespoon of sauce onto the ice cream in each glass, then follow with another scoop of ice cream. Pour the remaining sauce over the parfaits and sprinkle on the crushed malted milk balls.

Makes 2 parfaits

Opposite: Baked Alaska, page 176.
Preceding page: Baklava Parfait, page 96.

Eggnog Sundae

Ingredients

2 scoops Vanilla or Vanilla
   Custard Ice Cream
¼ cup brandy

¼ cup dark rum, preferably
   Myer's
ground nutmeg

Preparation

Place the ice cream in each of 2 dessert dishes. Add half the brandy and rum to each, then top with a sprinkling of nutmeg. Serve with wafers or rum balls, if desired.

Makes 2 sundaes

Flaming Fudge Sundae

Ingredients

4 scoops Chocolate Ice
    Cream
1 cup Hot Fudge Sauce

$^{1}/_{4}$ cup chocolate-flavored
    liqueur, such as
    Cheri-Suisse, Dröste,
    Sabra, or Vandermint
$^{1}/_{4}$ cup brandy

Preparation

Place a scoop of ice cream into each of 4 dessert dishes. Heat
the sauce in a small saucepan over low heat until it is very hot.
Stir in the liqueur and then add the brandy. Give sauce a
quick stir, then ignite the sauce and pour it, flaming, over the
ice cream.

Makes 4 sundaes

Photo 2 following page 122

Grasshopper Parfait

Ingredients

2 scoops Mint Chocolate
  Chip Ice Cream
¼ cup crème de menthe
¼ cup crème de cacao

½ oz. semisweet chocolate,
  chilled
sprigs of fresh mint

Preparation

Place 1 scoop of ice cream in the bottom of a parfait glass. Add 1 tablespoon crème de menthe and 1 tablespoon crème de cacao. Add another scoop of ice cream and the remaining liqueur.

Scrape shavings from the chocolate and sprinkle on top. Serve with sprigs of mint.

Makes 1 parfait

Photo 4 following page 170

Hot Banana-Pecan Sundae

Ingredients

½ cup butter
½ cup dark brown sugar
½ cup chopped pecans
2 medium-size ripe
  bananas, peeled and cut
  in ¼-inch slices

4 large scoops Vanilla,
  Butter Pecan, or Banana,
  Custard Ice Cream,
  slightly softened

Preparation

In a skillet over medium heat, melt the butter. Stir in the sugar and the nuts. Continue stirring for 5 minutes or until the sugar is dissolved. Add the bananas and cook 5 minutes longer, gently stirring. Remove from heat.

Place a scoop of ice cream in each of 4 dishes and top with banana-nut mixture.

Makes 4 sundaes

111

Irish Mist Parfait

Ingredients

1 ripe, fresh freestone peach
½ cup granulated sugar
2 scoops Vanilla Ice Cream
6 Tb. crème de cacao

2 scoops Cappuccino or
   Coffee Custard Ice Cream
6 Tb. Bailey's Irish Cream
candied coffee beans

Preparation

Peel and halve the peach, removing the pit. Slice the peach into ¼- to ½-inch sections, then roll each slice in the sugar until well covered. Place slices on a dish and chill for 1½ to 2 hours.

Place a scoop of Vanilla Ice Cream in each of 2 parfait glasses. Put 2 or 3 slices of peaches onto each ice cream scoop. Pour half the crème de cacao into each glass, then add a scoop of Cappuccino or Coffee Ice Cream to each. Add half the Bailey's to each parfait. Top with additional peach slices and garnish with candied coffee beans.

Makes 2 parfaits

Photo 4 following page 42

Jamaican Sunrise Parfait

Ingredients

2 scoops Mocha or Mocha
　Chip Ice Cream
2 Tb. Kahlua liqueur

1 Tb. tequila, preferably
　aged
whipped cream

Preparation

Place 1 scoop of ice cream into the bottom of a parfait glass. Add a tablespoon of Kahlua and follow with another scoop of ice cream. Pour on the remaining tablespoon of Kahlua and add the tequila. Top with a dollop of whipped cream and serve with almond cookies.

Makes 1 parfait

Maple Pecan Sundae

Ingredients

4 scoops Butter Pecan Ice
   Cream
$^1/_4$ cup maple syrup, warmed

$^1/_4$ cup dark brown sugar
$^1/_2$ cup pecan halves

Preparation

Place 2 scoops of ice cream in each of 2 large dessert dishes. Pour half the maple syrup onto each and sprinkle each with brown sugar. Scatter the pecan halves over the sundaes and serve.

Makes 2 sundaes

Photo 1 following page 154

Moonlight Cooler

Ingredients

4 scoops Lemon Custard Ice
  Cream
4 scoops Coconut Custard
  Ice Cream
½ cup Calvados or apple
  brandy

shredded coconut
4 candied lemon slices
  (optional)

Preparation

Place 1 scoop of each kind of ice cream into each of 4 sundae
dishes. Pour 2 tablespoons of Calvados onto each, and top
with shredded coconut. Garnish each sundae with a candied
lemon slice, if desired.

Makes 4 sundaes

Orange Cherry Jubilee

Ingredients

³/₄ cup extrafine sugar
³/₄ cup Curaçao or
　Cointreau liqueur
2 cups pitted and halved
　fresh sweet cherries

4 scoops Vanilla Custard Ice
　Cream
1 cup Kirsch
¹/₄ cup strips of orange zest
　(optional)

Preparation

Place the sugar and Curaçao or Cointreau into a saucepan set over moderate heat. Stir until the mixture is smooth and the sugar is dissolved, about 5 minutes. Remove from heat, add the cherries, and allow to steep for 3 to 4 hours.

Put a scoop of ice cream into each of 4 bowls. Spoon on the cherry-orange mixture. Warm the Kirsch in a small pan, then ignite it and carefully pour the flaming Kirsch over the sundaes. If desired, garnish with strips of orange zest.

Makes 4 sundaes

Photo 3 following page 170

Peach Melba Parfait

Ingredients

1⅓ cups Melba Sauce
8 scoops Buttermilk Peach
   Ice Cream

2 small, ripe freestone
   peaches

Preparation

Place 1 scoop of ice cream in each of 4 tall parfait glasses. Add 2 tablespoons of sauce to each, then follow with another scoop of ice cream for each glass. Drizzle on the remaining sauce.

Peel the peach and cut in half. Remove the pit, then slice the peach halves into ¼-inch slivers. Use the peach slices to decorate the tops of the parfaits.

Makes 4 parfaits

Photo 2 following page 26

Pousse Café Parfait

Ingredients

1 small scoop Vanilla Ice Cream
2 Tb. Blue Curaçao liqueur
1 small scoop Strawberry Ice Cream
2 Tb. Mandarine Napoleon liqueur

1 small scoop Mint Chocolate Chip or Lemon Custard Ice Cream
2 Tb. Chocolate Fudge Sauce

Preparation

Place a scoop of Vanilla Ice Cream in a tall parfait glass. Pour on the blue Curaçao, then place in the scoop of Strawberry Ice Cream. Add the Mandarine Napoleon liqueur and follow with the scoop of Mint Chocolate Chip or Lemon Custard Ice Cream. Add the fudge sauce and serve immediately.

Makes 1 parfait

Photo 4 following page 74

Rummy Sundae

Ingredients

2 scoops Rum Raisin Ice
   Cream
2 Tb. dark rum, preferably
   Myer's

1 Tb. eggnog mix powder
¼ cup Rum Raisin Sauce

Preparation

Place the ice cream in a large sundae dish. Add the rum, then sprinkle on the eggnog powder. Top with the sauce and serve immediately.

Makes 1 sundae

Photo 2 following page 186

Singapore Sling Sundae

Ingredients

4 scoops Cherry Vanilla Ice
   Cream
$1/4$ cup cherry brandy
2 Tb. gin

2 candied orange slices
2 mint sprigs

Preparation

Place 2 scoops of ice cream into each of 2 large sundae dishes. Add half the brandy to each, then half the gin. Garnish each sundae with an orange slice and a sprig of mint.

Makes 2 sundaes

S'more Sundae

Ingredients

6 graham crackers
1½ cups Chocolate Fudge
   Sauce

4 scoops Chocolate Ice
   Cream
½ cup Marshmallow
   Topping

Preparation

Place 1 graham cracker on each of 4 dessert plates. Spoon on about 1 tablespoon of sauce, then place 1 scoop of ice cream on top of each. Drizzle each ice cream scoop with about 2 tablespoons of topping. Spoon the remaining chocolate sauce over the sundaes. Crumble the remaining crackers and sprinkle the crumbs on the sundaes.

Makes 4 sundaes

Snow White Parfait

Ingredients

2 scoops Vanilla Custard Ice
  Cream
2 Tb. gin

2 Tb. Cointreau liqueur
orange peel (optional)

Preparation

Place 1 scoop of ice cream in a tall parfait glass. Add 1 table-spoon each of the gin and Cointreau, then follow with another scoop of ice cream. Add the remaining gin and Cointreau, then garnish, if desired, with a twist of orange peel.

Makes 1 parfait

Opposite: Tutti-Fruiti Charlotte, page 172.

Triple Strawberry Parfait

Ingredients

½ cup Strawberry Sauce
4 scoops Strawberry Ice
    Cream

¼ cup fraise de bois liqueur
whipped cream

Preparation

Place a tablespoon of sauce in the bottoms of 2 tall parfait glasses. Add a scoop of ice cream to each, then follow with another tablespoon of sauce to each glass. Place another scoop of ice cream in the glasses, and add 2 tablespoons each of the liqueur to each parfait. Top with the remaining sauce and serve with a dollop of whipped cream.

Makes 2 parfaits

Vienna Sundae

Ingredients

4 fresh, soft apricots, peeled
   and halved; or 8 canned
   apricot halves, drained
1/4 cup apricot brandy

4 scoops Vanilla or Coffee
   Custard Ice Cream
1/2 cup whipped cream
chopped hazelnuts

Preparation

Place the apricot halves in a small bowl with the brandy. Stir to coat well, then let sit for about 30 minutes.

Place an apricot half in the bottom of each of 2 tall parfait glasses. Add a scoop of ice cream, then put in another apricot half and a little of the soaking liquid. Add the remaining ice cream scoops and cover with the remaining apricots and liquid. Top with whipped cream and garnish with chopped nuts.

Makes 2 parfaits

Photo 2 following page 154

Strawberry Marshmallow Sundae

Ingredients

2 scoops Vanilla Custard Ice Cream

2 scoops Strawberry Ice Cream

$^1/_2$ cup Strawberry Sauce

$^1/_4$ cup Marshmallow Topping

2 fresh strawberries, washed and hulled

Preparation

In each of 2 sundae dishes, place a scoop of both ice creams side by side. Spoon on the sauce and then add the topping to each. Garnish sundaes with a fresh strawberry and serve.

Makes 2 sundaes

Opposite: Flaming Fudge Sundae, page 109.

Thanksgiving Sundae

Ingredients

2 scoops Spiced Cranberry
    Ice Cream
2 scoops Pumpkin Pie Ice
    Cream

1/2 cup Cranberry-Orange
    Sauce
chopped walnuts

Preparation

Place 1 scoop of the Cranberry Ice Cream into each of 2 sundae dishes. Add a scoop of the Pumpkin Pie Ice Cream and then spoon over the sauce. Garnish with chopped walnuts.

Makes 2 sundaes

Xerxes Sundae

Ingredients

4 scoops Buttermilk Peach
   Ice Cream
orange bitters
peach bitters

½ cup cream sherry
whipped cream

Preparation

Place 1 scoop of ice cream into each of 4 sundae dishes. Add a dash of orange and a dash of peach bitters to each, then spoon on 2 tablespoons of sherry for each dish. Top with whipped cream and serve.

Makes 4 sundaes

Sodas and Drinks

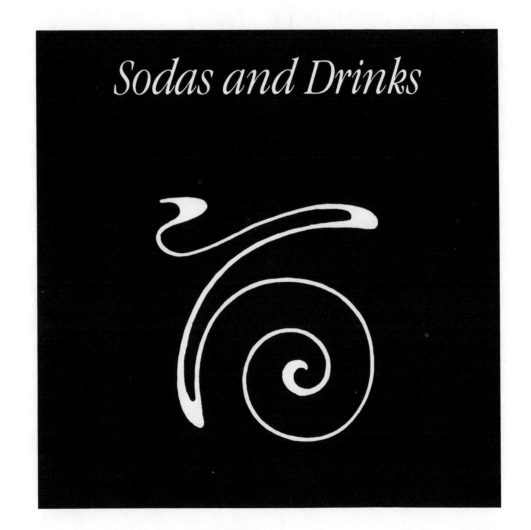

Vanilla Malted

Ingredients

2 large scoops Vanilla Ice
    Cream, slightly softened
3 Tb. Vanilla Syrup
1 cup very cold milk
1 Tb. malted milk powder
whipped cream (optional)
ground nutmeg

Preparation

In a blender—or the dispenser for a malted machine—place the ice cream, syrup, milk, and malt powder. If using a malt machine, mix for 1 minute; if using a home blender, blend on low speed for about 30 seconds.

Pour malted into a tall (10-ounce, if possible) glass until full and top with a swirl of whipped cream, if desired. Serve malted with a shaker of nutmeg for sprinkling on top and offer remaining mixture for refill.

Makes 1 soda

Photo 2 following page 106

Variation • Flavored Malted

This is the basic malted recipe. To make a chocolate or straw-berry malted, add 3 tablespoons of chocolate or strawberry syrup to the container along with the ice cream. For a change of pace, try one of the following:

- Banana, made with banana ice cream
- Butterscotch, made with butterscotch sauce and vanilla or butterscotch ice cream
- Cappuccino, made with coffee syrup and substituting ground cinnamon for the nutmeg
- Chocolate Mint, made with chocolate syrup flavored with 2 drops of peppermint extract or ¼ teaspoon crème de menthe
- Cinnamon Chocolate, made with cinnamon ice cream and chocolate syrup
- Cherry, made with cherry vanilla ice cream and cherry syrup
- Eggnog, made with vanilla ice cream and adding a whole egg to the container before blending; add a sprinkle of nutmeg and cinnamon
- Maple, made with maple syrup and vanilla ice cream
- Rum Raisin, made with rum raisin ice cream
- Strawberry, made with strawberry syrup and strawberry ice cream

Black and White

Ingredients

6 Tb. Chocolate Syrup
1/4 cup cold milk
4 cups chilled carbonated
   water
4 scoops Vanilla Ice Cream

Preparation

Place half the syrup in each of 2 tall soda glasses. Add half the milk to each glass and stir to loosely mix the syrup with the milk. Gently pour in the soda, mixing the syrup mixture with the water. Add 2 scoops of ice cream to each glass and serve.

Makes 2 sodas

Broadway Soda

Ingredients

¾ cup Chocolate Syrup
¾ cup cold half-and-half or milk
4 cups chilled carbonated water

4 scoops Coffee Custard Ice Cream
whipped cream

Preparation

Place 3 tablespoons of syrup in each of 4 soda glasses. Add 3 tablespoons of half-and-half and stir to blend well. Add about 1 cup of water to each glass, making a chocolate soda, then top each with a scoop of ice cream. Top with whipped cream.

Makes 4 sodas

Variation • Mocha Soda

Instead of chocolate syrup, substitute coffee syrup. Instead of coffee ice cream, use Extra-Bittersweet Chocolate Ice Cream.

Root Beer Float

Ingredients

*1 cold bottle (6 oz.) root
 beer
1 scoop Vanilla Ice Cream*

Preparation

Place the root beer in a chilled glass and add the scoop of ice cream. Do not stir.

For the Boston Cooler, a slight variation on the above, substitute strong, dry ginger ale for the root beer.

Makes 1 soda

Brown Cow

Ingredients

6 Tb. Chocolate Syrup
1 cup cold half-and-half or
   milk

2 chilled bottles (12 oz.
   each) good root beer
4 scoops Vanilla Ice Cream

Preparation

Place 1½ tablespoons of chocolate syrup into each of 4 tall soda glasses. Add ¼ cup of half-and-half to each and stir to blend the syrup. Add about half of each bottle of soda to each glass, then stir soda briefly and gently with a long-handled spoon. Top each soda with a scoop of ice cream and serve at once.

Makes 4 sodas

Strawberry Cooler

Ingredients

¼ cup Strawberry Syrup
4 scoops Vanilla Custard Ice
   Cream

1 chilled bottle (12 oz.) dry
   ginger ale
2 maraschino cherries

Preparation

Place half the syrup in each of 2 tall soda glasses. Add a scoop of ice cream to each and stir to blend the syrup slightly with the ice cream. Add ginger ale to each glass until about ¾ths full, then top off with remaining scoops of ice cream. Serve with a maraschino cherry on each.

Makes 2 sodas

Uptown Egg Cream

Ingredients

6 scoops Chocolate Ice
 Cream
2 cups cold milk
1 cup chocolate syrup
 (U-Bet, Hershey's, or syrup
 on page 192)

2 cups chilled carbonated
 water

Preparation

Place the ice cream, milk, and syrup in a blender and blend on low speed until smooth. Pour mixture into 6 tall glasses, filling each glass to about ⅔rds. Add the water to each, stirring gently so as not to allow the bubbles to escape. Serve with large stick pretzels.

Makes 6 sodas

Photo 2 following page 42

Banana Daiquiri

Ingredients

2 ripe medium bananas,
   peeled
1 cup light rum

1 pt. Banana Rum Custard
   Ice Cream, slightly
   softened
2 limes

Preparation

Cut 6 ¼-inch thick slices from one banana, then place remainder in the container of a blender. Add the rum and ice cream. Squeeze in the juice from 1 of the limes, then blend the mixture on medium speed until smooth, about 1 minute. Cut 6 ¼-inch thick slices from the remaining lime.

Pour the drink into 6 wide stemmed glasses and garnish each with 1 slice of lime and 1 slice of banana. Serve at once.

Makes 6 drinks

Opposite:Banana Daiquiri.
Following page: Baked Hawaii, page 178.

Brandy Alexander

Ingredients

1 pt. Cappuccino Ice Cream,
  slightly softened
2 Tb. brandy

2 Tb. crème de cacao
whipped cream
ground nutmeg

Preparation

Place the ice cream, brandy, and crème de cacao into the container of a blender and blend on medium speed until mixture is quite smooth. Pour into 2 tall glasses and add a dollop of whipped cream. Sprinkle with nutmeg and serve immediately.

Makes 2 drinks

Opposite: Black Berry Sundae, page 99.
Preceding page: Frozen Florida, page 140.

Frozen Florida

Ingredients

1 pt. Mandarin Orange
    Coconut Ice Cream,
    slightly softened
1 cup chilled milk
1 can (4 oz.) frozen orange
    juice concentrate

1 large egg
shredded coconut
orange slices (optional)

Preparation

Place the ice cream, milk, and orange juice concentrate in the container of a blender. Add the egg and blend on medium speed until the mixture is smooth, about 1 minute.

Pour into 6 tall stemmed glasses and top with shredded coconut. If desired, garnish each with a slice of fresh orange.

Makes 6 drinks

Photo 3 following page 138

Milk Punch

Ingredients

1 pt. Vanilla Custard Ice
   Cream
½ cup milk

¼ cup brandy
ground nutmeg

Preparation

Place the ice cream, milk, and brandy in the container of a blender. Blend until smooth, about 1 minute.

Pour mixture into 4 tall punch glasses and serve sprinkled with nutmeg.

Makes 4 drinks

Mint Julep Slush

Ingredients

1 pt. Peppermint Ice Cream,   4 sprigs fresh mint
    slightly softened
1 cup good-quality bourbon

Preparation

Place the ice cream and bourbon in the container of a blender and blend at low speed until smooth, about 1 minute.

Pour mixture into silver cups and garnish each with a sprig of mint.

Makes 4 drinks

Photo 2 following page 90

Panama Slush

Ingredients

1 pt. Vanilla Custard Ice
  Cream
½ cup dark rum, preferably
  Myer's

¼ cup crème de cacao
ground nutmeg

Preparation

Place the ice cream, rum, and crème de cacao in the container
of a blender. Blend on low speed until smooth, then pour
mixture into 4 tall glasses. Sprinkle each with some ground
nutmeg and serve.

Makes 4 drinks

Piña Colada

Ingredients

¹/₄ cup crushed pineapple
¹/₂ cup pineapple juice
¹/₂ cup light rum
2 Tb. coconut cream

2 scoops Vanilla Custard Ice
  Cream, slightly softened
4 fresh pineapple spears
  (optional)

Preparation

Place the pineapple, pineapple juice, rum, coconut cream, and ice cream in the container of a blender. Blend at medium speed until smooth, about 1 minute.

Pour the mixture into tall glasses and garnish, if desired, with pineapple spears.

Makes 4 drinks

Strawberry Daiquiri

Ingredients

1 pt. Strawberry Ice Cream
¼ cup crushed fresh
   strawberries or Strawberry
   Sauce
1 cup light rum

juice of 1 lime
3 strawberries, hulled,
   halved, and cut in fans

Preparation

Place the ice cream, strawberries, and rum in the container of a blender. Add the lime juice and then blend on medium speed until mixture is smooth, about 1 minute.

Pour the mixture into 6 wide stemmed glasses and garnish with strawberry fans. Serve immediately.

Makes 6 drinks

White Martini

Ingredients

2 scoops Vanilla Ice Cream
¼ cup gin

2 maraschino cherries
  (optional)

Preparation

Place the ice cream in the container of a blender and add the gin. Blend on medium speed until mixture is smooth.

Pour mixture into 2 martini glasses and garnish with a maraschino cherry, if desired. Serve at once.

Makes 2 drinks

Photo 2 following page 170

Whizz Doodle Slush

Ingredients

1 pt. Vanilla Custard Ice
  Cream
2 Tb. Scotch whiskey

2 Tb. crème de cacao
whipped cream

Preparation

Place the ice cream, whiskey, and crème de cacao into the container of a blender and blend on medium speed until mixture is smooth and foamy.

Pour into 4 tall glasses and top each with a swirl of whipped cream.

Makes 4 drinks

Cakes, Molds and Bombes

Cocoa Cherry Bombe

Ingredients

1 qt. Chocolate or Chocolate
  Malted Ice Cream
½ cup Chocolate Fudge
  Sauce

1 pt. Cherry Ice Cream
¼ cup sweetened cocoa
  powder
½ cup whipped cream

Preparation

Place a 6-cup ice cream mold into the freezer to chill for about 15 minutes. Remove the Chocolate Ice Cream from the freezer to soften slightly.

Pack the softened ice cream into the chilled mold to form a 1- to 1½-inch thick lining. You can smooth the ice cream into the mold and push it into the curves using the back of a large wooden spoon. Place in freezer to harden for about 2 hours.

Coat the curved inside of the ice cream with a ¼-inch layer of the sauce, then place the mold in the freezer to harden, about 1½ hours.

About 15 minutes before you are ready to remove the mold from the freezer, take out the Cherry Ice Cream to soften slightly. When mold is ready, spoon in the softened ice cream to fill the remaining area in the center of the mold. Cover ice cream with plastic wrap and return to freezer to harden for about 2 hours. Chill a serving plate.

To remove bombe from the mold, place the mold into a bowl filled with hot water for a few seconds, then invert bombe onto serving plate. Sprinkle outside of the bombe with cocoa powder, wipe edge of plate around the bombe clean, then pipe on rosettes of whipped cream.

To serve, slice crosswise with a sharp knife that has been dipped briefly in warm water. Before making each slice, dip the knife into the warm water again.

Makes about 8 servings

Photo 1 following page 186

Strawberry-Peach Bombe

Ingredients

1 qt. Buttermilk Peach Ice
   Cream
1 pt. Strawberry Ice Cream
1 small ripe peach

1 cup heavy cream, well
   chilled
2 Tb. peach brandy
½ cup Strawberry Cream
   Sauce

Preparation

Place an 8-cup mold in the freezer to chill for about 30 minutes. After about 15 minutes, remove the Buttermilk Peach Ice Cream from the freezer to soften slightly.

Pack the mold with a uniform 1- to 1½-inch layer of the peach ice cream, leaving a deep well in the center. Smooth the well with the back of a wooden spoon, then place the mold back in the freezer to harden completely, about 1½ hours.

About 15 minutes ahead, remove the Strawberry Ice Cream from the freezer to soften slightly. Pack a thin layer of this ice cream into the well, making about a ¾-inch layer. Smooth the well in the center and place mold back in freezer to harden, about 1½ hours.

While the bombe is hardening, bring a saucepan of water to a boil and immerse the peach for about 15 seconds. Remove and peel the peach, then cut in half and discard the pit. Chop the peach into small bits no larger than about ¼ inch; drain off excess juice. Set aside.

Whip the cream until stiff, then fold in the brandy and the peach bits. Pack the mixture into the center of the mold, cover with plastic, and place in freezer until firm, about 2 hours. Chill the serving plate.

To remove the bombe from the mold, place the mold into a bowl filled with hot water for a few seconds, then invert the bombe onto your serving plate. Pour over the sauce and serve at once.

Makes 8 to 10 servings

Peanut Brittle Mold

Ingredients

1 qt. Peanut Butter Ice
Cream

1 cup crushed peanut brittle
½ cup Hot Fudge Sauce

Preparation

Chill a 4-cup mold in the freezer for about 30 minutes.

About 10 minutes ahead, remove the ice cream from the freezer to soften slightly. Pack the mold with the ice cream, then place back in freezer to harden, about 2 hours.

To remove ice cream from the mold, place mold in a bowl filled with hot water for a few seconds, then invert ice cream onto serving plate. Dust outside of mold with the peanut brittle powder, pressing it into the ice cream to coat the entire mold evenly. Place back in the freezer to firm up the ice cream again, about 1 hour.

When ready to serve, heat the sauce. Remove mold from freezer and slice with a knife that has been briefly dipped into hot water. Place slices on individual plates and serve topped with hot fudge sauce.

Makes about 4 servings

Opposite: Maple Pecan Sundae, page 114.

Peppermint Snowballs

Ingredients

1 qt. Peppermint Ice Cream
1 cup shredded coconut

Preparation

Line a large baking sheet with waxed paper and place in freezer to chill for about 30 minutes.

About 5 minutes ahead, remove the ice cream from the freezer to soften slightly. Place individual scoops of ice cream on the baking sheet and put sheet back into the freezer to harden the ice cream balls, about 1 hour.

Spread the coconut on a sheet of waxed paper or in a shallow dish, and dip each of the ice cream balls into the coconut, turning the ice cream to coat the balls all around. Place the balls back on the baking sheet and put in freezer to harden again, about 1 hour more. Serve with peppermint sticks, chocolate sauce, or coconut macaroons.

Makes about 8 balls

Opposite: Vienna Sundae, page 126.

Chocolate Mint Bombe

Ingredients

2 oz. semisweet chocolate
1 Tb. butter
1 quart Chocolate Ice
 Cream
3 Tb. crème de menthe

1 pt. Mint Chocolate Chip
 Ice Cream
¼ cup heavy cream, well
 chilled

Preparation

Place a 4-cup mold in the freezer to chill for about 10 minutes. Meanwhile, place the chocolate and butter in a double boiler and set over hot, not boiling, water. Let chocolate melt, then stir to blend butter with chocolate.

Coat the inside of the mold with a thin layer of chocolate sauce, then place mold back into freezer to harden the chocolate. After about 30 minutes, chocolate should be hard.

About 15 minutes ahead, remove the Chocolate Ice Cream from the freezer to soften slightly. Remove the mold from the freezer and pack about 3 cups of the softened ice cream into the mold, making a 1-inch layer and leaving a well in the center. Place the mold back in the freezer to harden the chocolate layer, about 1½ hours. Place remaining ice cream back in freezer to use for another time.

About 10 minutes ahead, remove the Mint Chocolate Chip Ice Cream from the freezer to soften slightly. Remove the mold from the freezer and sprinkle into the center well about 2 tablespoons of crème de menthe. Then pack enough softened ice cream to fill the well completely. Smooth the top. Cover mold with plastic wrap and place back in freezer to firm, about 1½ hours.

To remove the bombe from the mold, place the mold into a bowl filled with hot water for a few seconds, then invert the bombe onto your serving plate. Smooth the top if there are any breaks or smears, then place briefly in the freezer to firm the chocolate layer if it got a little soft in the unmolding.

Whip the cream until it is almost firm, then add the remaining tablespoon of crème de menthe. Continue whipping until firm, then pack the whipped cream mixture into a pastry bag. Pipe rosettes of whipped cream around mold and serve at once, cutting wedges from the bombe with a knife that has been dipped briefly in warm water.

Makes about 4 servings

Photo 1 following page 58

Fruit Bonbons

Ingredients

½ cup finely chopped mixed candied fruit

2 Tb. Mandarin Napoleon liqueur

1 pt. Vanilla Custard Ice Cream

1 pt. Extra-Bittersweet Chocolate or Cinnamon Chocolate Ice Cream

8 oz. semisweet chocolate

¼ cup evaporated milk

¼ cup butter or shortening

Preparation

Place the candied fruit in a small bowl and add the liqueur. Let steep for about 2 hours, or until the fruit absorbs the liqueur.

Line a baking sheet with waxed paper and place in the freezer to chill for about 30 minutes.

Place a scoop of vanilla ice cream onto the sheet and make an indentation in the center. Place a little over 1 tablespoon of the fruit mixture into the center and then shape the ice cream around it, enclosing the fruit inside the ball of ice cream. Quickly repeat for the remaining 5 scoops of ice cream, using the remaining fruit mixture. Chill the ice cream balls if they appear to be melting.

Let the chocolate ice cream soften slightly, then take a scoop of it and flatten it. Wrap the layer of chocolate ice cream around the ball of vanilla ice cream, smoothing the outside and reshaping into a ball, if necessary. Continue for remaining vanilla ice cream balls. Set the balls onto the baking sheet and place sheet in the freezer to harden the ice cream, at least 4 hours.

Place the chocolate in a double boiler with the evaporated milk and shortening, and melt over hot, not boiling, water. Stir to blend well, then keep hot.

When the ice cream bonbons are very hard, take each between a fork and a spatula and dip into the melted chocolate to coat the outside completely. Work quickly, then transfer the chocolate-covered balls to the baking sheet and place back in the freezer to harden the coating, about 30 minutes more.

Makes 6 large bonbons

Photo 1 following page 42

Old-Fashioned Sugar Cones

Ingredients

2 large eggs, lightly beaten
½ cup granulated sugar
⅔ cup butter, melted and cooled

1 tsp. vanilla extract
½ tsp. almond extract
¾ cup all-purpose flour

Preparation

To make these cones you'll need a pizelle iron, a heavy hinged griddle normally used to make thin Italian wafer cookies.

In a mixing bowl, combine the eggs with the sugar and then stir in the butter. Add the extracts, then gradually sift in the flour until the mixture resembles a pancake batter.

Heat the iron until quite hot, then spoon on about 1½ tablespoons; the batter will spread to fill the grooves and make a cone about 5 inches in diameter. Close the iron and cook until golden; do not let the cones get too dark or they will be too crisp and will crumble when rolled. When done, remove the cone with a spatula and wrap snugly around a cone shape.

(You can fashion a cone from a piece of heavy brown paper.) There will be a slight overlap, making a cone about 2 inches wide at the broader end. Let cool briefly to hold shape, then slip off the cone mold and let cool completely.

After you've used about half the batter, it may have begun to thicken too much. Thin it back to the original consistency by adding 2 tablespoons of water.

When ready to use, place a scoop of desired ice cream into the cone. Unused cones can be stored in an airtight container for up to 2 weeks.

Makes about 12 cones

Note: Electric pizelle irons are available from Williams-Sonoma, P.O. Box 7456, San Francisco, CA 94120. Regular pizelle irons are sold in many specialty shops, especially those featuring baking supplies and Italian products.

Photo 1 following page 26

Ice Cream Cookie Cups

Ingredients

3 Tb. butter
⅓ cup granulated sugar
½ tsp. vanilla extract
2 large egg whites
½ cup all-purpose flour

1 qt. ice cream, any flavor
½ cup Apricot or Cherry
   Sauce
chopped nuts

Preparation

Preheat the oven to 375°. Generously grease a cookie sheet.

In a large bowl, cream the butter with the sugar. Add the extract and blend well. Beat the egg whites until stiff. Fold the egg whites into the butter-sugar mixture, then sift in the flour and fold gently to blend.

Spoon the batter onto the cookie sheet and spread to make circles about 8 inches in diameter; each of the wafer circles should be very thin—less than ⅛ inch thick. Bake for 5 minutes, or until slightly browned at the edges.

Immediately remove circles from the oven and shape them over the bottoms of glasses that are about 2½ inches in diameter. Make scallops on the sides so the cups have an undulating shape. Let them set for a minute or so, then remove, place upright, and let cool.

When ready to serve, place 1 scoop of ice cream into each cup and spoon over about 1 tablespoon sauce. Sprinkle with nuts and serve at once.

Makes about 6 cups

Chocolate Ice Cream Cups

Ingredients

8 oz. semisweet chocolate, chunked

2 Tb. butter

1 qt. Extra-Bittersweet Chocolate Ice Cream

1 cup heavy cream, well chilled

chocolate sprinkles

Preparation

Place the chocolate with the butter in a double boiler and melt over hot, not boiling, water. Stir to blend, then use a pastry brush to coat the insides of 8 to 10 paper muffin cups. Place cups in the freezer to harden the chocolate, about 30 minutes. Check the cups; if chocolate layer isn't thick enough (about ⅛ inch thick), then coat with another layer of chocolate and refreeze. When chocolate cups are hard, remove the paper liner and discard. Keep chocolate cups in freezer.

When ready to serve, place 1 scoop of ice cream into each of the cups. Whip the cream and top each cupcake with an "icing" of whipped cream. Scatter sprinkles on top of each and serve at once.

Makes 8 to 10 cupcakes

Fried Ice Cream

Ingredients

1 qt. Vanilla Ice Cream (or
   any other flavor)
1 cup finely crushed Rice
   Crispies (or graham crackers)

1 large egg
1½ Tb. milk
oil for deep-frying

Preparation

Line a baking sheet with waxed paper and then scoop out 8 individual balls of ice cream. Place ice cream balls on the baking sheet and place in freezer until firm, about 1 hour. Place cereal crumbs in a shallow bowl or on a sheet of waxed paper. Set aside. Mix the egg with the milk in a small bowl.

Remove ice cream from freezer and dip each ice cream scoop into the cereal crumbs, then into the milk-egg mixture, and back into the crumbs. Work quickly. Place coated balls on the baking sheet and freeze to firm coating, about 1 hour.

Heat the oil for frying to 375°. Drop 1 ball into the oil and fry for about 10 seconds, turning in the oil to brown all sides. Remove when coating darkens slightly and set aside briefly. Continue for remaining scoops and serve immediately.

Makes 6 servings

Photo 2 following page 58

Ice Cream Almond Fritters with Melba Sauce

Ingredients

1½ pt. Vanilla Custard Ice Cream
1 cup slivered almonds
½ cup finely crushed vanilla wafers or graham crackers

1 large egg
1 cup Melba Sauce
2 Tb. framboise liqueur
oil for deep-frying
1 cup fresh raspberries

Preparation

Line a baking sheet with waxed paper and place in freezer to chill for about 15 minutes.

Make 12 small scoops of ice cream and place onto the baking sheet. Put sheet in freezer to harden the ice cream, about 30 minutes. In a shallow pan or on a sheet of waxed paper, stir together the slivered almonds and crushed cookies. In a small bowl, lightly beat the egg.

Remove the ice cream balls from the freezer and dip each first into the beaten egg and then into the crumb-nut mixture.

Place back on baking sheet and chill in freezer until firm, about 30 minutes.

Heat the sauce in a double boiler or heavy saucepan and add the liqueur. Keep warm.

Heat the oil to 375° and then drop the fritters in a few at a time. Turn in the oil and fry for only about 5 seconds, then remove and place on a serving dish, 3 fritters to a serving.

Drop the raspberries briefly into the sauce, then pour the sauce and raspberries over each of the servings of fritters. If desired, serve with whipped cream.

Makes 4 servings

Photo 3 following page 74

Ice Cream Cookie Sandwich

Ingredients

2 oz. unsweetened chocolate
½ cup butter or margarine
1 cup granulated sugar
1 large egg, lightly beaten
¼ cup evaporated milk
1 tsp. vanilla extract

2½ cups all-purpose flour
pinch of salt
2 tsp. baking powder
2 pt. Vanilla Custard Ice
  Cream
4 oz. semisweet chocolate,
  melted (optional)
2 Tb. evaporated milk

Preparation

Preheat the oven to 350°. Place the chocolate in a double boiler and melt over hot, not boiling, water. Let cool slightly.

Place the butter in a large mixing bowl and cream with the sugar. Add the egg and mix well, then add the evaporated milk, melted chocolate, and vanilla.

In a separate bowl, sift together the flour, salt, and baking powder. Add the flour mixture to the wet mixture, blending

168

well. If mixture is sticky, chill in refrigerator for about 30 minutes, or until firm and easy to handle.

Roll dough out onto a floured surface until about ¼ inch thick and cut 3-inch cookies with a round biscuit cutter. Reroll dough and cut remaining cookies. Place on a greased cookie sheet and bake for about 15 minutes or until the cookies are firm to the touch. Cool on a rack.

Remove the ice cream from the freezer to soften slightly, then spread about ½ cup of ice cream onto each of 12 cookies. Top each with another cookie and place in freezer to chill. (You may have additional cookies left over; save them for another use.)

If desired, heat the chocolate with the evaporated milk in a double boiler and dip each of the chilled sandwiches in the sauce to coat all or partially with chocolate. Chill again and serve frozen.

Makes about 12 sandwiches

Lemon Custard Pie

Ingredients

1 cup graham cracker
  crumbs
¼ cup butter, melted
1 qt. Lemon Custard Ice Cream

1 cup heavy cream, chilled
3 Tb. confectioners sugar

Preparation

Mix the crumbs with the melted butter until moist. Spread the mixture in a 9-inch pie pan and press until smooth. Chill for about 30 minutes.

Remove the ice cream from the freezer to soften slightly. Spoon the ice cream into the shell, smoothing the top and packing in well. Cover with plastic wrap and put in freezer to harden, about 1 to 2 hours.

In a large bowl, whip the cream until light and fluffy. Gradually add the sugar and whip until stiff. Pack the cream into a pastry bag and pipe a latticework topping on the pie. Trim the edge with rosettes of whipped cream and serve.

Makes about 8 servings

Opposite: Lemon Custard Pie.
Following page: White Martini, page 146.

Campfire Pie

Ingredients

1 cup chocolate cookie
   crumbs
¼ cup butter, melted
1 qt. Marshmallow Vanilla
   Ice Cream

1⅓ to 1½ cups
   Marshmallow Topping
1 Tb. brandy, warmed

Preparation

Mix the cookie crumbs with the melted butter until moist. Spread the mixture in a 9-inch pie pan and press until smooth. Chill for about 30 minutes.

Remove the ice cream from the freezer to soften slightly. Spoon the ice cream into the shell, smoothing the top and packing in well. Cover with plastic wrap and put in freezer to harden, about 1 to 2 hours.

When ready to serve, spoon the topping over the pie and then sprinkle the brandy on top. Ignite the brandy and serve flaming.

Makes about 8 servings

Opposite: Grasshopper Parfait, page 110.
Preceding page: Orange Cherry Jubilee, page 116.

Tutti-Frutti Charlotte

Ingredients

1 dozen ladyfingers, split in half
1 qt. Tutti-Frutti Ice Cream
1 can (14 oz.) whole canned sweet cherries, drained

1 cup Cherry Sauce
1 cup heavy cream, whipped

Preparation

Line the bottom and sides of a 6-cup charlotte mold with the ladyfingers. Place the rounded sides toward the mold; you'll have to cut some of the ladyfingers to fit them tightly into the mold and get them to meet at the center. Trim any that extend beyond the edge of the mold.

Remove the ice cream from the freezer to soften slightly, then spoon the ice cream into the mold, pressing it against the ladyfingers. Continue until the mold is full, then smooth the top and cover with plastic. Return to the freezer and chill for 2 to 4 hours or until the ice cream is hard.

To remove charlotte from the mold, invert mold onto your serving dish. Cake should release very easily.

Garnish the charlotte with the drained cherries and pour sauce over. If desired, pipe rosettes of whipped cream around and serve with additional whipped cream.

Makes about 6 servings

Photo 1 following page 122

Mocha Ice Cream Layer Cake

Ingredients

1 qt. Extra-Bittersweet Chocolate Ice Cream

1 qt. Coffee Custard Ice Cream

1 qt. Vanilla Malted Ice Cream

1 cup heavy cream, chilled

¼ cup sweetened cocoa powder

¼ cup chopped walnuts

Preparation

The following directions are provided for those with only 1 or 2 cake pans. If you have 3, you can prepare the 3 layers all at once.

Remove the chocolate ice cream from the freezer about 15 minutes ahead to allow to soften slightly. When softened, spread in an 8-inch round cake pan. Cover with plastic wrap and place in freezer to firm, about 2 hours.

Remove the coffee ice cream from the freezer to soften slightly. Dip the cake pan with the chocolate ice cream into a bowl of hot water and invert the ice cream layer onto your serving plate. Place chocolate layer back in freezer. Rinse the cake pan and dry well. Spread the coffee ice cream in the pan. Cover with plastic wrap and place in freezer to harden, about 2 hours.

Remove the vanilla ice cream from the freezer to soften slightly. Dip the cake pan with the coffee ice cream into a bowl of hot water and invert the ice cream layer on top of the chocolate layer on the serving plate. Place the cake back in the freezer. Rinse the cake pan and dry well. Spread the vanilla ice cream in the pan. Cover with plastic wrap and place in freezer to harden, about 2 hours.

Dip the cake pan with the vanilla ice cream into a bowl of hot water and invert the ice cream layer on top of the coffee layer. Place cake back in freezer until you are ready to decorate it.

Whip the cream until stiff, then fold in the cocoa. "Ice" the cake with the whipped cream and sprinkle with the nuts. Serve at once.

Makes about 8 servings

Baked Alaska

Ingredients

2 cups cake flour
2 tsp. baking powder
½ cup butter
1½ cups granulated sugar
4 large eggs, separated
¾ cup milk

1 tsp. vanilla extract
1 qt. each Vanilla,
   Chocolate, and Strawberry
   Ice Cream
¼ tsp. cream of tartar

Preparation

Preheat the oven to 350°. Grease an 8-inch round cake pan.

In a medium mixing bowl, sift the flour once, then measure and sift again with the baking powder. Set aside.

In a large mixing bowl, cream the butter and then add 1 cup of sugar. Cream until light and fluffy. Add the egg yolks, blending well after adding each one. Add the flour, alternating with the milk, and beat until smooth. Add the vanilla and stir. Pour batter into the cake pan and bake for about 50 minutes or until cake springs back in the center.

Let cake cool for about 10 minutes in the pan, then remove from pan and let cool completely on a rack.

If you have more than 1 layer pan, you can prepare a couple of the ice cream layers at once. For each layer, allow the ice cream to soften slightly, then spread 4 cups of the ice cream in an 8-inch cake pan and place in the freezer to firm up, about 2 hours.

Place the cake on a foil-lined baking sheet. Dip the chocolate ice cream layer pan in hot water for a few seconds, then unmold onto the cake layer. Follow with the vanilla layer and then the strawberry layer. If you only have 1 or 2 cake pans, then place cake and ice cream layers into freezer until you are able to assemble the entire Baked Alaska. When all layers are assembled, place cake back in freezer to harden for about 2 hours.

Preheat the oven to 450°.

In a large mixing bowl, beat the egg whites with the cream of tartar until they form soft peaks. Gradually add the remaining sugar, then beat until the whites form stiff peaks. Spread the meringue over the cake, covering the top and sides. Make swirls and little peaks to decorate the cake. Bake cake for 5 minutes, or until the meringue begins to brown. Transfer cake to a serving dish and serve at once.

Makes about 10 servings

Photo 4 following page 106

Baked Hawaii

Ingredients

1 small Hawaiian pineapple
¼ cup Kirsch
½ cup chopped macadamia
   nuts
1 pt. Banana Custard Ice
   Cream

¼ cup shredded coconut
3 large egg whites
¼ tsp. cream of tartar
⅓ cup granulated sugar

Preparation

Make sure the pineapple is completely ripe; it should be soft and have an appetizing pineapple scent. Cut it in half lengthwise, retaining the tops for decoration if possible. Scoop out the flesh and discard the core. Chop the pineapple flesh and mix it with the Kirsch in a small bowl. Set aside to macerate for about 2 hours.

Preheat oven to 450°. Line a baking sheet with aluminum foil.

Place a sprinkling of nuts into each of the pineapple shells. Add 2 scoops of ice cream to each, then add the soaked pineapple pieces. Pour over any juices, then sprinkle with more nuts and the coconut.

In a large mixing bowl, beat the egg whites with the cream of tartar until they form soft peaks. Gradually add the sugar and beat until the whites form stiff peaks. Spread the meringue over the 2 shells, swirling the top to make patterns whose edges will brown. Place pineapples on the baking sheet and put into oven to brown for about 5 minutes. Remove and serve at once.

Makes 2 large servings

Photo 2 following page 138

Apricot-Nut Ice Cream Roll

Ingredients

¾ cup cake flour
¾ tsp. baking powder
¼ tsp. salt
4 large eggs
¾ cup extrafine sugar

1 tsp. vanilla extract
1 qt. Hazelnut or Butter
   Pecan Ice Cream
1 cup Apricot Sauce

Preparation

Sift the flour once, then combine with baking powder and salt and sift again. Set aside.

Preheat the oven to 400°. Grease a 10 × 15-inch jellyroll pan, then line with waxed paper. Grease paper and dust lightly with flour.

Place the eggs into a bowl that is set over a larger bowl of hot water. Using an electric mixer, beat the eggs and add the sugar gradually until the mixture becomes thick and light colored. Remove bowl from the hot water and add the vanilla, then fold in the flour mixture. Pour the batter into the prepared pan and bake for about 10 or 12 minutes or until center springs back when tested.

Remove cake from the oven and let stand a few minutes, then invert carefully onto a clean dish towel. Remove paper from bottom and trim crisp edges. While still warm, roll up in the towel and let cool.

About 15 minutes ahead, remove ice cream from freezer and let soften slightly. Unroll the cake and spread the ice cream in an even layer about ½ inch thick. Reroll the cake and place on a baking sheet, then put in the freezer to harden, about 2 hours.

When ready to serve, prepare sauce and then cut slices of the roll using a knife that has been warmed briefly in hot water. Pour over the sauce and serve at once.

Makes about 8 servings

Chocolate Gingerbread Ice Cream Roll

Ingredients

½ cup + 3 Tb. extrafine sugar
1 cup all-purpose flour
1 tsp. baking soda
¼ tsp. salt
3 eggs, separated
¼ cup butter, melted
¼ cup molasses

¼ cup unsweetened cocoa powder
2 Tb. ground ginger
1 Tb. ground cinnamon
3 Tb. water
1 qt. Chocolate Ice Cream
whipped cream
confectioners sugar

Preparation

Preheat the oven to 375°. Lightly grease a 10 × 15-inch jelly-roll pan, then line it with waxed paper. Grease the waxed paper and sprinkle it with 3 tablespoons each of the sugar and flour. Sift together the remaining flour, baking soda, and salt. Set aside.

Place the eggs into a bowl that is set over a larger bowl of hot water. Using an electric mixer, beat the eggs and add the sugar gradually until the mixture becomes thick and light colored. Remove bowl from the hot water and add the melted butter, molasses, cocoa, ginger, cinnamon, and water. Fold in the flour mixture.

Beat the egg whites until stiff, then fold into the batter. Pour the batter into the prepared pan and bake for about 10 to 12 minutes, or until the center is firm to the touch. Let cake cool for about 1 minute, then turn out onto a clean kitchen towel. Peel off the waxed paper and trim the crisp edges of the cake. Roll the cake up in the towel and let cool.

When ready, remove the ice cream from the freezer to soften slightly. Unroll the cake and spread about a 1-inch layer of ice cream onto the cake. Reroll the cake and place on a baking sheet. Put in the freezer to harden, about 2 hours.

When ready to serve, transfer the roll to your serving dish and sprinkle with confectioners sugar. Slice into 1-inch pieces, using a knife that has been warmed briefly in some hot water. If desired, serve with whipped cream.

Makes about 8 to 10 servings

Photo 2 following page 74

Chocolate Pecan Pie

Ingredients

½ cup graham cracker
   crumbs
½ cup finely chopped
   pecans
¼ cup butter, melted

1 qt. Butter Pecan Custard
   Ice Cream
6 oz. semisweet chocolate
2 Tb. evaporated milk
12 pecan halves

Preparation

Mix the graham cracker crumbs and nuts with the melted butter until moist. Spread the mixture in a 9-inch pie pan and press until smooth. Chill for about 30 minutes.

Remove the ice cream from the freezer to soften slightly. Spoon the ice cream into the shell, smoothing the top and packing in well. Cover with plastic wrap and put in freezer to harden, about 2 hours.

Melt the chocolate with the evaporated milk in a double boiler over hot, not boiling, water. Stir to blend well, then pour over the ice cream in the shell to coat the top. Press in the pecan halves and return to freezer to harden, about 1 hour.

Makes about 8 servings

Toppings, Sauces and Syrups

Chocolate Sauce

Ingredients

3 oz. unsweetened chocolate
2/3 cup butter
2 cups granulated sugar
pinch of salt

1 cup light cream or
   half-and-half
1 tsp. vanilla extract

Preparation

Place the chocolate and butter in a double boiler and heat over hot, not boiling, water. Stir the mixture as the chocolate melts, then gradually add the sugar and the salt. Blend well, continuing to heat over hot water, and add the cream. Stir, then remove from heat. When cool, add the vanilla.

Store sauce in an airtight container in refrigerator until ready to use. Sauce may thicken slightly; to use, heat in double boiler until of pourable consistency.

Makes about 2 cups

Opposite: Cocoa Cherry Bombe, page 150.

Chocolate Fudge Sauce

Ingredients

¾ cup granulated sugar
½ cup unsweetened cocoa
   powder
¾ cup light corn syrup

2 Tb. butter
pinch of salt
1 tsp. vanilla extract

Preparation

Place the sugar and cocoa in a double boiler and stir well. Add the corn syrup, and blend until the mixture is uniformly moist. Place over hot, not boiling, water and heat the mixture until the sugar is dissolved and sauce is smooth. Gradually add the butter, blending well, and add salt. Let cool, then add the vanilla. This sauce is best for making vanilla fudge or other chocolate swirl ice creams.

Makes about 2 cups

Opposite: Rummy Sundae, page 119.

Hot Fudge Sauce

Ingredients

¼ cup butter, cut up
4 oz. unsweetened
   chocolate, cut up
¾ cup granulated sugar

½ cup heavy cream
pinch of salt
1 tsp. vanilla extract

Preparation

Place the butter and chocolate in a double boiler over hot, not boiling, water. Heat until melted, then stir in the sugar gradually so that sugar dissolves. Add the cream and blend well. Place briefly over the hot water and continue to heat until mixture is very hot and sauce is smooth. Add salt, then remove from heat. Let cool briefly, then add the vanilla and serve hot.

Makes about 2 cups

Chocolate Mousse Sauce

Ingredients

2 oz. semisweet chocolate
2 Tb. butter

¾ cup heavy cream
1 tsp. vanilla extract

Preparation

Place the chocolate and butter in a double boiler over hot, not boiling, water until melted. Stir well, then add ¼ cup of the cream and stir again. Let cool to room temperature. Stir in the vanilla.

Whip the remaining cream until stiff, then fold into the chocolate mixture. Serve at once.

Makes about 2 cups

 *Chocolate Syrup*

Ingredients

2 cups granulated sugar
1½ cups water

1 cup unsweetened cocoa
    powder
2 tsp. vanilla extract

Preparation

Place the sugar and water in a heavy saucepan and bring to a boil. Reduce heat to medium and cook, stirring constantly, until mixture is clear and syrupy, about 8 minutes. Add the cocoa gradually, stirring to blend, then remove from the heat and let cool. When cool, add the vanilla. Store in an airtight container until ready to use.

Makes about 3 cups

Butterscotch Sauce

Ingredients

1 cup light brown sugar
2 Tb. light corn syrup
2 Tb. butter

½ cup heavy cream
½ tsp. vanilla extract

Preparation

Place the sugar, syrup, butter, and cream in a saucepan over moderate heat and bring to a boil. Cook, stirring constantly, until the mixture thickens, about 235° on a candy thermometer. Remove from heat and let cool. Add the vanilla.

Store sauce in an airtight container in refrigerator until ready to use. Serve cold, or reheat in a double boiler.

Makes about 1½ cups

# Caramel Sauce

Ingredients

1½ cups granulated sugar
¾ cup water, heated to
  boiling

¼ cup heavy cream
1 tsp. vanilla extract

Preparation

Place the sugar in a saucepan over moderate heat. As sugar just barely begins to melt, lower heat to a bare simmer and stir constantly until the sugar turns golden brown. Continue stirring over low heat until it becomes medium dark brown. Gradually stir in the boiling water until well blended, then heat over moderate heat until thickened slightly. Remove from heat and add the cream and vanilla. Serve hot or cold.

Makes about 2 cups

# Coffee Sauce

Ingredients

1 cup granulated sugar
1 cup water
2 Tb. instant coffee powder

2 Tb. butter
½ cup heavy cream

Preparation

Place the sugar and water in a heavy saucepan and set over medium-low heat. Cook, stirring constantly, for about 5 minutes, or until the sugar has melted and you have a clear, smooth syrup. Add the coffee, stir to dissolve, then remove from the heat. Gradually stir in first the butter, then the cream, blending well. Store sauce in an airtight container in refrigerator until ready to use.

Makes about 2 cups

# Coffee Syrup

Ingredients

½ cup dark brown sugar
½ cup dark corn syrup
1 cup water

2 Tb. instant coffee powder
dissolved in ¼ cup water

Preparation

Place the sugar, corn syrup, and water in a heavy saucepan and bring to a boil. Reduce heat to medium and cook, stirring constantly, for 5 minutes. Remove from the heat and add the coffee mixture. Blend well and set aside to cool. Store in airtight containers until ready to use.

Makes about 1½ cups

Vanilla Syrup

Ingredients

1 vanilla bean, split
1 cup granulated sugar

1 cup water

Preparation

Place the vanilla bean, sugar, and water in a heavy saucepan and bring to a boil. Reduce the heat to medium and stir constantly to dissolve the sugar as the mixture boils for 5 minutes. Remove the vanilla bean and let cool. Store syrup in an airtight container until ready to use.

Makes about 1 cup

Cinnamon Sauce

Ingredients

³/₄ cup granulated sugar
¹/₄ cup dark corn syrup
¹/₂ cup water

2 cinnamon sticks, broken
    in half

Preparation

Place the sugar, corn syrup, and water in a heavy saucepan over medium-low heat. Bring mixture to a boil and stir to dissolve the sugar. Add the cinnamon sticks and simmer over low heat for 10 minutes. Cool, then remove cinnamon and place sauce in an airtight container until ready to use.

Makes about 1 cup

# Ginger Sauce

Ingredients

½ cup fresh ginger, peeled
  and cut into small pieces
½ cup dark brown sugar

½ cup water
½ cup dark corn syrup
¼ cup half-and-half

Preparation

Place the ginger in a heavy saucepan along with the sugar and water. Bring to a boil over medium-high heat, stirring to dissolve the sugar. Reduce heat and simmer for about 20 minutes, or until ginger is soft. Remove the ginger pieces and discard. Add the corn syrup and stir over medium heat for about 2 or 3 minutes, then add the half-and-half. Cool and store in an airtight container in refrigerator until ready to use.

Makes about 1 cup

Marshmallow Topping

Ingredients

1 cup granulated sugar
½ cup water
2 cups miniature
   marshmallows

½ tsp. vanilla extract
1 egg white

Preparation

Place the sugar and water in a saucepan and bring to a boil. Boil for about 5 minutes, or until mixture is syrupy. Add the marshmallows and stir until marshmallows melt and blend with syrup. Add the vanilla and let cool slightly.

Beat the egg white until very stiff, then fold into the marshmallow mixture. Serve at once.

Makes about 2 cups

Chestnut Sauce

Ingredients

¾ cup granulated sugar
1 cup water

½ cup chestnut puree
   (available in cans from
   specialty food shops)
1 teaspoon vanilla extract

Preparation

Place the sugar and water in a heavy saucepan and bring to a boil. Stir to dissolve the sugar, then cook for 5 minutes over medium heat until the mixture is clear and syrupy. Remove from the heat and gradually stir in the puree and vanilla. Blend well, then store in an airtight container until ready to use.

Makes about 2 cups

Maple-Walnut Topping

Ingredients

1 cup dark maple syrup
½ cup chopped walnuts

2 Tb. butter

Preparation

Place the maple syrup in a heavy saucepan and gently heat until almost a boil. Simmer for about 5 minutes, or until thickened slightly. Remove from heat and stir in the walnuts, then gradually add the butter, blending well. Serve hot.

Makes about 1¼ cups

Rum Raisin Sauce

Ingredients

½ cup dark raisins
¾ cup dark rum, preferably
   Myer's

1 cup granulated sugar
½ cup water
¼ cup butter

Preparation

Place the raisins in a bowl with half the rum. Let soak for 1 hour, or until plumped. Drain and set aside.

Put the sugar with the water into a heavy saucepan and bring to a boil. Stir to dissolve the sugar, then cook over moderate heat for 5 minutes, or until the mixture is darkened and syrupy. Remove from heat and add the remaining rum and the soaked raisins. Gradually stir in the butter, and set aside to cool.

Makes about 1½ cups

Apricot Sauce

Ingredients

1 cup chopped dried
  apricots
1½ cups water

1 cup granulated sugar
1 Tb. Kirsch or Cointreau
  liqueur

Preparation

Place the apricots in a bowl. Heat ½ cup of water to almost boiling, then pour over the apricots. Let soak for about 30 minutes, or until plumped. Place the mixture in a blender and whirl for about 1 minute, or until mixture is a smooth puree.

Place the remaining water and the sugar in a heavy saucepan. Bring to a boil, then stir and cook over moderate heat for about 5 minutes, or until mixture is clear and syrupy. Add the apricot puree, then remove from heat. Let cool slightly, then add the liqueur. Store in an airtight container until ready to use.

Makes about 1½ cups

Cherry Sauce

Ingredients

1 cup good cherry jam
¹/₄ cup water
juice of 1 lemon

1 Tb. butter
1 Tb. flour

Preparation

Place the jam in a heavy saucepan and add the water and lemon juice. Place over very low heat until jam melts. Stir to blend with the water.

Melt the butter in a small saucepan, and stir in the flour. Blend well, then stir mixture into the warm jam mixture. Cook over low heat until smooth. Serve hot or store for later use.

Makes about 1¹/₂ cups

Cherry Syrup

Ingredients

2 cups fresh pitted sweet
   cherries, chopped

$^1\!/_2$ cup water
2 cups granulated sugar

Preparation

Place the cherries in a saucepan with the water and bring to a boil. Simmer for 5 minutes, then strain through very fine cheesecloth or linen into a bowl. Push the cherries to extract their juices, but for the clearest juice, do not push the fruit mush too hard. Transfer the juice to a saucepan and add the sugar. Bring to a boil and boil for 5 minutes, or until mixture is syrupy. Store in an airtight container for later use.

Makes about 2 cups

Cranberry-Orange Sauce

Ingredients

1 cup chopped fresh
   cranberries
1 cup water

zest of 1 large orange,
   chopped
¾ cup granulated sugar

Preparation

Place the cranberries in a heavy saucepan with ½ cup of water and ½ cup of sugar. Bring to a boil over high heat, then reduce heat to medium and cook until berries are softened and liquid is syrupy, about 8 minutes. Crush the berries to mash them into the syrup.

Bring the zest and remaining water and sugar in a boil in another saucepan and then simmer over moderate heat for about 5 minutes. Combine orange sauce with cranberry sauce and let cool until ready to use.

Makes about 2 cups

Melba Sauce

Ingredients

1 pt. fresh raspberries   ½ cup granulated sugar

Preparation

Place the raspberries in a blender along with the sugar. Whirl until you have a puree, about 1 minute. If desired, you can remove the seeds from the sauce by pressing the puree through a fine sieve. This sauce should be used within 24 hours.

Makes about 2 cups

Pineapple Topping

Ingredients

1 large ripe pineapple   ¾ cup granulated sugar

Preparation

Peel and core the pineapple, then chop the pulp into ½-inch pieces. Put half the pineapple into a blender or food processor and puree the mixture. Place the puree in a heavy saucepan and add the sugar. Bring to a boil over high heat, then reduce heat to moderate and cook for about 10 minutes, or until the mixture is syrupy. Remove from heat and add remaining pineapple pieces. Chill the sauce and then serve within 24 hours.

Makes about 3 cups

Strawberry Cream Sauce

Ingredients

1 cup sliced strawberries
1/2 cup granulated sugar

1/2 cup heavy cream

Preparation

Place the strawberries in a bowl with the sugar and let macerate for 2 hours.

Whip the cream until stiff, then fold in the strawberries and liquid. Blend well, and serve immediately.

Makes about 2 cups

Strawberry Syrup

Ingredients

1 cup fresh strawberries, sliced

½ cup granulated sugar

Preparation

Place the strawberries in a blender or food processor and puree until smooth. Transfer the puree to a heavy saucepan and add the sugar. Bring to a boil over high heat, then reduce the heat to medium and boil, stirring constantly, for about 5 minutes or until mixture is thick and syrupy. Remove from the heat and strain through a fine sieve to remove the seeds if desired.

Makes about 1 cup

Strawberry Topping

Ingredients

1½ cups sliced fresh
strawberries

1 cup granulated sugar
½ cup water

Preparation

Place the sugar and water in a heavy saucepan and bring to a boil over high heat. Reduce heat to medium and cook for 5 minutes, or until mixture is smooth, clear, and syrupy. Remove from heat and add the strawberries. Let stand for 30 minutes, then gently stir to break up some—but not all—of the berries. Chill and serve within 24 hours.

Makes about 2 cups

Conversion Tables

The following are conversion tables and other information applicable to those converting the recipes in this book for use in other English-speaking countries. The cup and spoon measures given in this book are U.S. Customary (cup = 236 mL; 1 tablespoon = 15 mL). Use these tables when working with British Imperial or Metric kitchen utensils.

Liquid Measures

The Imperial pint is larger than the U.S. pint; therefore note the following when measuring the liquid ingredients.

U.S.	IMPERIAL
1 cup = 8 fluid ounces	1 cup = 10 fluid ounces
½ cup = 4 fluid ounces	½ cup = 5 fluid ounces
1 tablespoon = ¾ fluid ounce	1 tablespoon = 1 fluid ounce

U.S. MEASURE	METRIC*	IMPERIAL*
1 quart (4 cups)	950 mL	1½ pints + 4 tablespoons
1 pint (2 cups)	450 mL	¾ pint
1 cup	236 mL	¼ pint + 6 tablespoons
1 tablespoon	15 mL	1+ tablespoon
1 teaspoon	5 mL	1 teaspoon

*Note that exact quantities are not always given. Differences are more crucial when dealing with larger quantities. For teaspoon and tablespoon measures, simply use scant or generous quantities; or for more accurate conversions, rely upon metric.

Solid Measures

Outside the U.S., cooks measure more items by weight. Here are approximate equivalents for basic items in this book.*

	U.S. CUSTOMARY	METRIC	IMPERIAL
Apples (peeled and chopped)	2 cups	225 g	8 ounces
Butter	1 cup	225 g	8 ounces
	½ cup	115 g	4 ounces
	¼ cup	60 g	2 ounces
	1 tablespoon	15 g	½ ounce
Chocolate chips	½ cup	85 g	3 ounces
Coconut (shredded)	½ cup	60 g	2 ounces
Fruit (chopped)	1 cup	225 g	8 ounces
Nut Meats (chopped)	1 cup	115 g	4 ounces
Raisins (and other dried fruits)	1 cup	175 g	6 ounces

*So as to avoid awkward measurements, some conversions are not exact.

	U.S. CUSTOMARY	METRIC	IMPERIAL
Sugar (granulated)	1 cup	190 g	6½ ounces
	½ cup	85 g	3 ounces
or caster	¼ cup	40 g	1¾ ounces
(confec-	1 cup	80 g	2⅔ ounces
tioners) or	½ cup	40 g	1⅓ ounces
icing	¼ cup	20 g	¾ ounce

Index